THE LIBRARY AND INFORMATION PROFESSIONAL'S GUIDE TO THE INTERNET

Third Edition

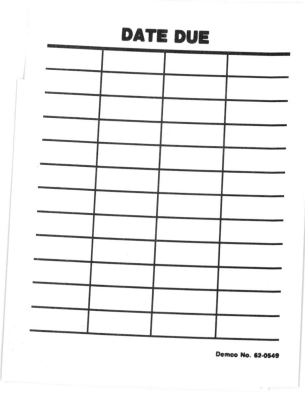

DATE DUE

Demco No. 62-0549

THE LIBRARY AND INFORMATION PROFESSIONAL'S GUIDE TO THE INTERNET

Third Edition

Alan Poulter
School of Information Management, Leeds Metropolitan University

Debra Hiom
Institute for Learning and Research Technology, University of Bristol

Gwyneth Tseng
Formerly of the Department of Information and Library Studies, Loughborough University

LIBRARY ASSOCIATION PUBLISHING
LONDON

© Alan Poulter, Debra Hiom and Gwyneth Tseng, 2000

Published by
Library Association Publishing
7 Ridgmount Street
London WC1E 7AE

Library Association Publishing is wholly owned by The Library Association.

First published 1996
Second edition 1997
This third edition 2000

British Library Cataloguing in Publication Data

A catalogue record for this book is available from the British Library.

ISBN 1-85604-376-2

Typeset in 11pt Aldine 401 and Chantilly from authors' disks by Library Association Publishing.
Printed and made in Great Britain by MPG Books, Bodmin, Cornwall.

Contents

Preface to the Third Edition

It is quite frightening to look back at the changes made to the second edition and realize that they now look dated, after only two years. The changes made in this edition have been no less radical than then. This edition has seen a rewrite of much of the text and a reorganization of most sections. For example, in the section on e-mail we now look at e-mail viruses, what to do about spam and how to handle attachments. Resource Guide entries have been streamlined, to allow more entries, and a whole new category on 'Portals and e-business' has been added. Illustrative screen dumps have been dropped, as they date faster than text.

In particular in this edition we have attempted to include:

- the latest developments in connecting to the Internet in terms of new technology (ISDN, ADSL, cable modems etc) and new services (free ISPs, 'free' dial-up etc).
- new web technology, specifically on how clientside programs (Java, etc) work, multimedia plug-ins and helpers, web cams, streaming TV and radio services, and more.
- more depth of coverage in searching the web, by discussing meta search engines, how to find special types of data like images or sounds, how to search newsgroup and mailing list archives and explaining the use of metadata.
- recognition of the commercialization of the Internet, with material on 'portals' and their personalizable services, and the advantages and pitfalls of online shopping and auctions.
- new 'advanced' topics like diagnosing browser and networks faults, understanding more about domains and their ownership and more.

Once again, to aid the reader in navigation, terms defined in the text are printed in **bold** and text references to resources listed in the Resource Guide are *italicized*.

Finally, the Resource Guide from this edition will be available in an abbreviated form on the web itself, as part of an ongoing effort to support the book and keep the text up to date with current developments. Purchasers of this book will be able to register for access to this site at **http://www.lapwing.org.uk**

Alan Poulter
School of Information Management,
Leeds Metropolitan University

Debra Hiom
Institute for Learning and Research Technology,
University of Bristol

Gwyneth Tseng
Formerly of the Department of Information and Library
Studies, Loughborough University

Preface to the First Edition

Communication is a cornerstone of human society and the early 1990s have seen the take-off of a new communications phenomenon – the Internet. Internet has become the buzzword of the nineties. Open a professional journal, or the technology pages of a newspaper and the Internet is probably mentioned somewhere. Even TV and radio series have been devoted to it.

The Internet is a vast network of interconnected computers which spans the globe. Since 1987 it has seen an unprecedented growth which has far outstripped that of any other computer network in existence. At the time of writing there are nearly 16 million machines and 66 million people with at least electronic mail access to the network, and the number is growing daily. Indeed, the growth in usage of the Internet, however measured, is now so rapid that it is virtually impossible to quantify – statistics are out of date as soon as they are produced. The rate of development of new Internet products and services is simply staggering.

The Internet began life as an academic and research network, supported by US government finance, and for many academics and government sponsored researchers it has now established itself as a resource as vital to their work as the word processor, telephone or fax. It provides them with hitherto unparalleled free access to data and information in the form of databases, software, computing resources, reports, electronic texts, games and much more (as well as access to fee-based services too). But perhaps its greatest asset is the connection to millions of other users, providing the opportunities to communicate, disseminate and seek information with people across the world. In more than 186 countries, academics, scholars, researchers and students are using it, on a massive scale, to do just that.

In the early 1990s the Internet became widely available to private users and businesses in the USA, and this trend is now taking off in the UK and elsewhere. Whether or not the Internet survives this rapid commercialization in its current form, it undoubtedly offers a vision of a future in which computer mediated communication and information delivery will be as common-place in developed societies as the telephone and TV today. It is a phenomenon that simply cannot be ignored by the information and library community if it is to shape the 'Internet' of the future.

But if the scale of the Internet is overwhelming, hardly less so is the variety of different types of information and communication facilities it offers and the whole new vocabulary it has spawned. Faced with a bewildering array of 'information at your fingertips' it is difficult to know where and how to begin. How do you find something that could be, almost literally, anywhere in the world? 'Cyberspace' contains a great deal of information that is of little or no value or interest to the vast majority of its inhabitants. How do you locate what is useful and relevant without wasting time searching through a morass of useless data?

We have produced this book as a launching pad into the world of the Internet for librarians and information professionals, academics and students who are new to networking. We hope too that Internet veterans will find the book a useful reference.

Part I gives a brief technical background and a history of the Internet. It explains the development of academic networking in the UK and looks at what the future may hold. Part II outlines what the Internet offers and how it can be used, concentrating on features that are likely to be of particular interest to library and information professionals. This part assumes no previous knowledge or experience of the Internet. Part III covers more advanced techniques for getting the most out of the Internet and the major tools that facilitate location and retrieval of information. Throughout, procedural instructions are purposefully kept to a bare minimum; this is not intended as a step-by-step guide to using various tools. There are so many tools and they change so fast that such coverage would be of limited use and quickly become out of date. Instead, we have attempted to provide just enough information to get started without overwhelming new users with too much, or unnecessarily duplicating what has already been published elsewhere. Since so many new terms have been coined to describe Internet facilities, we have emboldened these terms in the text as we introduce and define them.

The last major section of this book is a Resource Guide in which we have *very* selectively identified freely available Internet services which are either specifically aimed at the library and information community or offer good coverage of particular types of electronic information. These provide leads to electronic conferencing systems and journals, to general and subject-based collections of information, to library OPACs and information services, and to network information, training materials and software. We have also included special sections that lead to information from publishers, booksellers and the media, commercial online information retrieval services, government and related institutions, and relevant professional associations. Close to our own hearts, there is also a section on resources for library/information educators and trainers.

Unlike most of the other published Internet guides, our focus is on resources of most interest to UK readers although this does not restrict the coverage to UK materials only. To try to avoid the rapid obsolescence problem on the Internet, we have only quoted and referenced resources which, in our opinion, will be around for the foreseeable future. Resources are grouped into categories and each entry gives a short description, along with details of how to access it. Where a particular resource is available via a variety of different routes or systems, a UK or European option is presented first.

Obviously we can only give a *very* small selection from an almost incomprehensible wealth of materials. The other problem is that Internet services and facilities are changing and growing, quite literally, by the hour. That is the nature of the Internet – it would not be as exciting if it were not constantly improving and expanding. We have tried to concentrate on resources that are well-established. Where there are good 'meta-resources' or regularly updated directories or listings of electronic journals, OPACs and the like, we have pointed readers to these rather than attempting to reproduce their contents. With these as a starting point we hope that with time and enthusiasm to explore the Internet, readers will be able to hunt out and use resources for themselves. Whatever your professional interests or personal hobbies, someone else somewhere on the Internet shares them!

Gwyneth Tseng and Alan Poulter
Department of Information and Library Studies,
Loughborough University of Technology

Debra Hiom
Institute for Learning and Research Technology
University of Bristol

PART 1
Networking fundamentals

Contents

Introduction 2

Introduction to Part I

Part I introduces the Internet – what it is and what it can be used for. It explains some of the technical terms that every Internet user needs. It outlines the history of the Internet, explains where the UK academic network, JANET, fits in, and takes a glimpse at the future of networking. The user is also referred to Part 4, the Resource Guide, where a section on networking organizations lists some UK, European and international organizations that are good sources of up-to-date information on network developments.

Chapter 1

BACKGROUND AND HISTORY OF THE INTERNET AND UK NETWORKS

What is the Internet . . . ?

The first networks linking computers began to emerge as early as the 1940s. Not until the 1970s, however, did it become cost-effective and reliable for ordinary computer users to transmit data between computers over long distances. Today there are thousands of networks worldwide. There are five basic types according to their purpose and administration:

- **Academic** – established, normally with government support, for use by members of the academic and research community. These networks generally serve a region or a country. Examples include **BITNET** in the USA and **JANET** in the UK.
- **Corporate** – in-house proprietary systems, linking staff and machines at a single site and/or between branches and divisions of a company or organization; these are normally private with tight security to restrict access to authorized members of the organization.
- **Cooperative** – where the costs are supported by a group of separate institutions or individuals. Many cooperative cataloguing systems, whereby member libraries could exchange catalogue records, were originally established on this basis. In contrast, FidoNet is a global network of ordinary microcomputers maintained and run by computer hobbyists. In fact, FidoNet has nodes (ie connection points) in most countries of the world.
- **Commercial** (for-profit networks) – available to the public at large, or to closed user groups, on a fee-paying basis. A prime example is *AOL*, an American network with a global user-base, which has added a range of UK-specific information to its services in order to attract more British users.
- **Metanetworks** – these are 'networks of networks' encompassing any or all of the above types; the Internet is a metanetwork – a vast conglomerate of interconnected computer networks that brings together people, information and computer resources across the globe.

What makes the Internet more important than any other network now in existence is its overwhelming number of users – estimated at 195 million with Internet access in September 1999, with predictions of over 300 million by 2005 (source: *NUA Internet Surveys*). It is by far the world's largest metanetwork, with nothing to match it in terms of the number of sites connected and number of active users. From its genesis, its critical mass of users in the academic community was sufficient to secure its success. Now, in over 200 countries worldwide, it is available to virtually the whole academic community – staff, students and administrators alike – for no charge at point-of-use (though the introduction of bandwidth charging in the UK may change this in the future, and of course not all the facilities on the Internet are freely available). Recent 'open door' policies in several countries, allowing private individuals and organizations to make relatively low-cost connections, have established the Internet as the de facto standard for international networking. An estimated one-third of all homes in the USA have a PC, many of these with Internet connections. The number of commercial sites connected has now overtaken the number of academic sites. The mid-1990s saw a flood of UK companies making their first, trial Internet connections, following an inexorable trend in the USA. The UK now comes second only to the USA (though admittedly a long second) in terms of the number of host computers connected – nearly 1.6 million in July 1999 (source: *Internet Domain Survey*) . Although Internet access is still restricted to the academic sector in some countries, a global user-base is now emerging which once was fragmented between a large number of disparate networks.

. . . and what does it offer?

Coupled with the growth in the number of users, the ever-increasing sophistication, reliability and speed of computer-to-computer networks have spawned a completely new form of human communication – so-called **computer mediated communication** (CMC). Whereas the telephone and the broadcast media offer one-to-one and one-to-many communication respectively, the Internet offers a new dimension, namely many-to-many communication whereby groups and individuals can communicate with each other worldwide. Although the Internet is still nowhere near as pervasive as the telephone, radio or TV, it is giving rise to a new, mass communications culture, empowering groups who share a common interest not only to communicate among themselves, but to disseminate ideas, propaganda and information to wider audiences: in effect, groups and individuals can easily become publishers, lobbyists, advertisers, retailers, consultants and more. The strong ethos of freely sharing information has, to a large extent, been responsible for the Internet's meteoric growth. Commercial systems, like AOL, have not grown anything like as fast and, after offering their users access to free Internet resources, have had to reduce charges to compete.

The Internet today gives access to an overwhelming amount of information, data and electronic information services provided by its ordinary users. At one end of the spectrum there are personal 'home pages' published by people the world over (for a name-searchable collection see *Ahoy: The Homepage Gateway*). At the other end is official government information, for example that provided by the **open.gov.uk** website, which provides a first point of entry for all UK government and public sector information.

To give a few examples, the Internet can be used to:

- exchange personal messages with colleagues, friends or relatives at other networked sites
- engage in group discussions, exchange information and ideas with people who share a common interest, and seek information from them
- automatically receive information on world events, leisure interests, and technical, business, and professional matters by subscribing to electronic journals, conferences, newsletters and alerting services
- look up information in reference works, databases and libraries worldwide
- retrieve journal articles, books, computer programs and graphic images, and transfer them to a personal computer
- make use of computer facilities that are not available locally
- download new software or updates for existing applications
- browse catalogues of goods and services and make credit-card purchases
- participate in distance learning and academic conferencing
- engage in real-time 'chat' and multi-player interactive games
- communicate with individuals or groups by means of voice only or voice and image
- publish information for access by other Internet users.

Virtually anyone can use the Internet to look for information with only a minute or two's training – but 'cyberspace' (as it has become known) is a vast place to wander. To use many of its facilities purposefully, it is necessary to become familiar with some basic procedures and concepts.

Some networking terminology explained
LANs, WANs and network connections

The two basic types of network are **local-area networks** (LANs) and **wide-area networks** (WANs). A LAN links computers that are physically close to each other and usually 'hard wired' together via cables. Typically, LANs are used in single organizations at single sites. WANs, however, can cover large distances, within and beyond national boundaries; they are generally connected through telecommunications links, which may use a mixture of advanced technologies such as fibre-optic cables and satellites. It is the wide-area networks that are of most concern here.

Computers handle digital data in the form of discrete bits (binary digits, taking one of two values) and bytes (groups of 8 bits, taking 256 values). Networks transmit data in one of two forms, either analogue (a continuous signal) or digital (a stream of bytes). Most networks, like the Internet, use dedicated digital telecommunications lines. Organizations that make heavy use of an external network may install leased telecommunications lines to provide permanent digital links from their in-house multi-user machines or LANs to external network services. Individual and private users make a dial-up connection to an **access provider** via ordinary telephone lines. This is almost invariably an analogue connection and requires translation of data between analogue and digital forms. This translation is done by a **modem**.

Bandwidth

Dedicated network lines, especially if they are made of **optical fibre**, can handle far more data than can an ordinary telephone line, even using the latest, fastest modems. The limit on data transfer, the **bandwidth** of a telecommunications line, can still be reached even on the fastest of lines when lots of users try to move vast amounts of data. In the UK, the Internet noticeably slows down during the day as Americans start using it in ever-increasing numbers throughout their daylight hours.

Protocols

Networks require a common framework of routines and rules to allow computers to communicate with each other. These are called **protocols**. Protocols are technically complex, but very simply put they specify, for example, how data are to be encoded for transmission, the physical transmission media that are allowable, the conventions for addressing items of data so that they can be delivered to the correct network destination, and the applications (the types of tasks) that are to be supported on the network.

A variety of protocol suites has emerged both in proprietary networks, as for example IBM's system network architecture (**SNA**) and also in academic networks with **TCP/IP** (transmission control protocol/Internet protocol) for the Internet and the Coloured Book protocols on the original JANET service. The **OSI** (open systems interconnection) reference model, first proposed by the

CCITT (then the **Consultative Committee on International Telegraphy and Telephony**), was an attempt to impose international standardization, but has never achieved universality. A variety of different protocols continues to proliferate, although more and more users are moving to TCP/IP.

Networks using different protocols need a method of exchanging data. This is done through **gateway** services, which effectively 'translate' data from one set of protocols to another. Some gateways are more sophisticated than others. Ideally, the user should not be aware that the gateway exists: in other words, the commands and operating procedures on either side of the gateway, and the facilities offered, are, from a user's point of view, identical. Such gateways are said to be **transparent** or **seamless**.

Packet switching

Most WANs (including the Internet) use **packet switching** techniques. The first to do so were **X.25** networks. A protocol breaks a message down into small packets. Each packet includes some of the data from the message, together with a sequence code identifying where those data fit into the complete message. Each packet also has an address of the recipient computer and an address for the sending computer. Packets are totally hidden from users.

There are many advantages to using packets. They can be routed in a variety of ways between sender and recipient computers, thus bypassing any network failures or bottlenecks. Packets can be received in any order, as the sequence codes enable the original message to be re-assembled. A recipient computer can check the sequence codes of packets it receives to work out if any have been lost. The main disadvantage of packets is that they cannot handle (easily) information that must be delivered in 'real time' (ie according to timing restrictions). Thus sound or video can be transmitted across networks like the Internet, but a user will notice jerkiness in playback.

The client/server model

Any use of a network involves at least two computers: the one the user is on, and another one that is being accessed for some purpose via the network. The user's computer may be a personal computer directly connected to the network, or a multi-user **network host** to which the user connects from their own machine, which acts as a terminal. Some networks, like FidoNet, operate on the **peer-to-peer** model. This means that no one computer is more important than any other. However, most networks, the Internet among them, operate the **client/server** model. One computer, the client, on behalf of the user, requests services of another computer, the server. The speed and power of the server, and the bandwidth of the network connection, determine how quickly these services are fulfilled. At any one time a server computer can be dealing with any number of client computers. Thus server computers tend to be more powerful than client computers, whose job very often entails merely the display of data passed along from a server.

This split between client and server is matched by a split in the functions of network software. A database, for example, might consist of a server program, which stores and retrieves data, and a client program, which generates the requests for data and displays the results. Each part of the system can be optimized for its job. The client program, for example, might operate using a **graphical user interface** (with mouse, windows and icons), to make things easy for the user. The server program would need no such adornments. Finally, the server and client programs can run on completely different makes and types of computer, which allows the formation of heterogeneous networks like the Internet, which can connect a user on an archaic IBM PC XT with a Cray supercomputer.

The development of the Internet in the USA

Essentially, the Internet is a group of networks that use the TCP/IP sets of protocols to communicate. More meaningfully, the Internet is the world's largest computer network – actually, a global network of smaller university, government, corporate and commercial networks, which are linked directly or through more-or-less seamless gateways to (originally) government-financed national 'backbone' services. As far as users are concerned, the networks function almost as though they were one. They provide a pool of resources that can be reached from anywhere in the network.

The history of the Internet is a story that has been told many times, but a brief overview is necessary to understand the character and functioning of the Internet today.

Its origins lie in **ARPANET** (Advanced Research Projects Agency Network), which was commissioned in 1969 by the US Defense Department to provide a secure communications channel for US military research which would be resilient to nuclear attack. From the outset, therefore, the network was decentralized, so that it could continue to function if any part were destroyed. ARPANET proved so successful that in 1983 the military use was split off and the remaining service opened up to other researchers. At that point, ARPANET connected 60 universities in the United States, one in Norway and two in the United Kingdom. By the following year, over 1000 **host computers** were connected.

The opening up of ARPANET to a wider academic cohort coincided with the genesis of desktop computing. Network links from personal computers to campus mainframes, acting as Internet hosts, were established – vastly increasing the potential user group.

As more and more institutions and networks connected to ARPANET, the term internetworking (hence, Internet) evolved, but ARPANET itself soon became a bottleneck. In 1985 the National Science Foundation (NSF) organized the funding of five supercomputer centres at university sites around the USA. These supercomputers provided a new **backbone** to what was known as **NSFnet**, which offered vastly improved transmission speeds, capable of handling far more data traffic. The old ARPANET was gradually phased out. In the USA, regional networks were created and linked to the backbone. NSF policy was to allow anyone with an academic or research affiliation to use the network at little or no cost – indeed, campus connections were only funded if there was a local policy to provide broad access to the network for all members of the institution.

In 1987 a contract to manage the NSFnet was awarded to **Merit Network, Inc**, a non-profit consortium of eight Michigan universities. Funding was provided by the NSF and the State of Michigan, with commercial sponsorship for improved lines and equipment. Other national networks were encouraged to connect, and commercial users started to gain access. Today the Internet links together national backbone services, intermediate-level wide-area networks (both public and private) and private institutional local-area networks.

National and global information infrastructures

The visions of the Clinton administration are for a **National Information Infrastructure** (NII) in which every home, business and school in the USA can eventually access the network, and a commitment from governments worldwide to create a powerful and universal **Global Information Infrastructure** (GII) with open competition enshrined in its use. The earliest expression of these visions was the **National Research and Education Network** (NREN) a high-speed network first introduced by the then US Senator Albert Gore in 1990, and approved by the House of Representatives toward the end of 1991. Currently the big projects are **Internet2** (I2) and the **Next Generation Internet** (NGI). The former is a collaborative effort between over 150 US universities to develop advanced Internet technology and applications vital to the research and education missions of higher education. Internet2 is working to enable applications such as telemedicine, digital libraries and virtual laboratories that are not possible with today's Internet speeds. The latter initiative is a Federal research and development programme that is working on advanced networking technologies, developing revolutionary applications that require advanced networking, and demonstrating these capabilities on testbeds that are 100 to 1000 times faster than today's Internet. These initiatives are intended to overlap and share resources.

The development of the Internet in the UK

JANET

JANET (Joint Academic Network) is the UK academic network. Its origins lie in several small scientific networks that were developed in the UK from the late 1960s onwards; for example, the National Physical Laboratory's network established in 1968. However, JANET's direct forerunner was the Science and Engineering Research Council Network, **SERCnet**. Many university and former polytechnic sites were connected to SERCnet through switching centres at the Rutherford Appleton Laboratory, Daresbury Laboratory and the universities of London, Cambridge and Edinburgh.

During the 1970s the Computer Board, which funded university computing services at that time, was looking to rationalize the existing UK networks and build a national backbone service. A series of investigations resulted in the formation of the **Joint Network Team (JNT)** in 1979 to spearhead developments. SERCnet was to be used as the basis of the new network, but it also integrated other Research Council networks.

JANET was inaugurated on 1 April 1984. It is now funded by the **Joint Information Systems Committee (*JISC*)** of the Higher Education Funding Councils and managed by the **UK Education and Research Networking Association (UKERNA)**, which has taken over the responsibilities of the JNT.

All UK universities are connected, as are Research Council establishments and other national bodies such as the British Library, the National Library of Wales and the Imperial Cancer Research Fund. An increasing number of colleges of further education are also establishing JANET links. Affiliated membership is available to tertiary-level colleges. A few commercial organizations that collaborate with academic institutions are also connected – for example, Blackwell, which handles journal subscriptions for many academic libraries. By and large, though, the JANET user-base is still very firmly centred on the UK academic community, and its purpose is to support education and research.

JANET and the Internet

The Coloured Book protocols developed for the original JANET X.25 service could not be interworked with TCP/IP, so an Internet gateway was provided at the Rutherford Appleton Laboratory, with a direct fibre-optic link to NSFnet being opened in 1987. In 1991 JANET was directly linked to the Internet via the **JANET IP Service (JIPS)**. This allows TCP/IP and X.25 data to run over the JANET backbone. Now JANET usage is IP-based.

SuperJANET

Just as the USA is seeking to upgrade its networks for high-performance computing, so too is the UK. In fact, work on implementing the UK high-performance academic network, SuperJANET, is well advanced. Unlike the US, though, there are
no plans for SuperJANET to become a commercial venture. Funding for
SuperJANET was announced at the end of 1992 (£5 million per year for four years).
The aim was to upgrade transmission speeds. This meant a huge investment in re-
cabling to upgrade the existing network infrastructure – not only the backbone, but
also network links right through to the user's desktop. SuperJANET II started during 1995. It was aimed at significantly increasing the spread of SuperJANET, and
helped to create a number of metropolitan area networks (MANs), linking geo-
graphically close universities; 12 MANs were created in all. SuperJANET III was
aimed at consolidating the pioneering work of SuperJANET and SuperJANET II.
At the time of writing tenders are out for SuperJANET IV.

The future of networking: 'Information superhighways'

Upping network transmission speeds is not merely a question of coping with an
increasing number of users. Even more significantly, high-speed networks will
allow the real-time transmission of **multimedia** data – voice, image and video
communications as well as text. In 1994, video pictures were first transmitted
across the Internet, but far greater network bandwidth is required for images than
for straight text. As the volume of multimedia traffic increases, current technologies will be inadequate – hence the pressing need to implement the so-called
information superhighways like SuperJANET and NREN/Internet2/NGI.

A UK national superhighway?

The cost of installing a nationwide fibre-optic network to every home, office,
school and hospital in the UK would run into billions of pounds. Cable companies have made a start, but the development is piecemeal and targeted towards
lucrative market-sectors. The government has already been urged by an all-party
committee of MPs to open the way for BT to build a national high-speed network
in the UK. Unlike SuperJANET, this would be available to everyone, not just academics and researchers. The committee's recommendation was that the current
entertainment restrictions on BT and Mercury, which protect cable TV companies from competition, should be removed in order for BT to generate revenue to
help finance the project.

What the future holds is still very uncertain, but a vision is certainly there of
converging technologies for communication, information and entertainment services to homes and offices throughout the land.

UK libraries and the Internet

There is a great deal of interest into researching and building digital or electronic libraries. In the summer of 1995, *JISC* announced funding for a range of projects under the *Electronic Libraries Programme* (eLib). This was a direct response from the UK higher education funding bodies to exploit networking to help alleviate pressures on academic library resources, as student numbers and worldwide production of information spiral inexorably upwards. There are several programme areas, including **on-demand publishing** projects that look at supplying reading materials in electronic format to whole classes of students and examining the flexibility of access, as well as licensing and copyright arrangements. A variety of **electronic journals**, some incorporating multimedia, have been developed and investigated in terms of impact on authors and readers, the economics of publishing and so forth. **Electronic ordering** and **document delivery** services will continue to be developed in an effort to cut the cost and delivery times of interlibrary loans. Not least, some of the projects aim to enhance the awareness and expertise of academic and library staff in using network resources and exploiting them appropriately. The Programme is now in its third and final phase, which is concentrating on bringing a range of technologies together in **hybrid library** projects and looking at large-scale resource discovery through the development of **clumps**. This third phase is also taking some of the more successful projects from phases 1 and 2, such as the **subject gateways** funded under the access to network resources strand, and trying to help them move forward into becoming self-supporting services.

JISC is also jointly funding a number of collaborative digital library projects with the National Science Foundation: the first six projects were announced in the summer of 1999 and will involve researchers in the UK and the US working together in areas such as **cross-domain resource discovery**, **digital preservation** and **citation linking**. Other UK initiatives include the Digital Library Research Programme of the *Library and Information Commission* (the LIC is soon to become part of the new Museums, Libraries and Archives Council). In the public library sector *EARL* is developing the **UK Electronic Library**, which will provide electronic content and act as a gateway to Internet resources for public libraries. More generally the **National Grid for Learning** (NGfL) aims to provide access to learning on the Internet for a variety of sectors.

Commercialization of the Internet

Paying users needed to be brought onto the network in large numbers to help finance the considerable research and development for the NII. In 1994 the NSF announced that it was awarding contracts to commercial telecommunications companies to operate four new **Network Access Points** (NAPs) on the high-speed backbone. Previously, the backbone was reserved for traffic from educational and research institutions, with traffic from commercial sites on the Internet being routed via private, revenue-generating carriers. The NSFnet backbone was decommissioned in April 1995, entirely replacing the government-sponsored service with a fully commercial system of backbones.

At the time this issue was the subject for much speculation on discussion groups across the network. In the rush to encourage private-sector involvement, the future of the public-sector infrastructure was seen to be under threat. Many people were worried that usage-based fees would replace the moderate subscriptions paid by many private users and that the current flexibility of the administration and openness of the system would be undermined. These fears have, however, proved unfounded.

One particular issue that still highlights the conflict between public and private interests is the furore that rages around the question of advertising. The Internet is used for advertising and there are conventions which define what is acceptable and what is not. However, for-profit activities and extensive use of the Internet for private and personal business were originally considered to be unacceptable by the NSF – and indeed this is still the case for those with academic accounts on the Internet. Blatant advertising is still considered to be unacceptable by many Internet users. Inevitably, though, commercial concerns increasingly look to the Internet fraternity as a new mass market for their goods and services. **E-commerce**, the buying and selling of products and services via a network, has really taken off recently. The incredible success of companies like Amazon.com have ignited a virtual 'gold rush' for businesses around the world seeking profits from new networked forms of production, retailing and distribution. Governments are also concerned about e-commerce, both how to regulate it and also how to foster it. *Electronic Commerce and the European Union* is an excellent source for information in this area.

Inexorable commercialization of the Internet may seem to point to an insecure future for its hitherto open and free communications infrastructure, but that is to underestimate the critical mass that the Internet has already achieved, the commitment of its users and the extraordinary rate of development of new products and services. Wherever the balance between public and private interests eventually falls, there is every reason to believe that the Internet will have an ever-increasing impact on education, businesses and homes. The culture of the Internet is at odds with commercial realities, where information has a price tag and commercial interests need to be protected.

Internet culture

The Internet is unusual in that it is not centrally owned, controlled or managed.

Operators of participating networks cooperate to maintain the infrastructure, with one or two steering committees to coordinate improvements. The most influential of these come under the auspices of the *Internet Society*, an international body made up of volunteers. This makes for a very dynamic system which is continually offering more and better features through the efforts and contributions of its enthusiastic user community. The *World Wide Web Consortium* (*W3C*) is an international industry consortium led by the creator of the web, Tim Berners Lee. The consortium works towards providing non-proprietary specifications and software for the web.

Possibly because of its origins in US academic and research circles, the Internet has developed into a very open, democratic system in which free speech is respected (though not protected by international law); in theory at least, every user has an equal opportunity to be heard. The Internet has spawned a culture of cooperation and low-cost exchange of ideas, data and software hitherto unknown on such a scale.

Not everything about this culture is rosy, however, and negative aspects (like child pornography, bomb-making instructions and sexual harassment) have been extensively reported in the media. The Internet reflects the people that use it. A handful of people use the Internet for things that the vast majority of users do not approve of: this is not a problem intrinsic to the Internet but simply brought about by the existence of antisocial individuals in society. Contrary to popular opinion fostered by the traditional media, which have yet to grasp the workings of the Internet, the Internet is not awash with illicit software, pornographic images or stolen credit-card details.

Chapter 2
CONNECTING TO THE INTERNET

Getting a connection to the Internet
Internet access providers

Your organization may already provide you with Internet access (as at academic sites, for example). Alternatively you can pay a commercial **Internet service provider** (ISP), some of which offer low-cost connections aimed at individual users, while others specialize in linking corporate networks, with a range of options (and costs) in between. Essentially an individual user needs a telephone socket connected to a computer with a **modem** (a device which enables computer signals to traverse a telephone line). The modem, under the control of **communications software**, calls a number which, once user identification and a password have been given, opens a connection into the Internet. Just about any sort of computer sold by a computer dealer for business or home office use can be used to access the Internet. This is known as **dial-up** access. For a listing of ISPs see the *InetUK: UK Access Providers* site.

A recent development in the UK has been the appearance of so-called 'free' ISPs, which do not charge for their services, including the British Library, which is one of the first public-sector bodies in the UK to offer a free Internet service. The free ISPs have special telephone numbers for dial-up Internet access from which they receive a share of the telephone connection charge. They have expanded the number of home Internet users drastically, at the cost perhaps of offering a less than reliable service. In response, some of the charging ISPs are offering free connection time. To further complicate matters, since modems have reached a ceiling in terms of speed, new technologies like **ISDN** (Integrated Services Digital Network), are now being offered to home users. The home user currently faces a very difficult task in choosing between all these competing options. The *uk.telecom FAQ* is a great source of knowledgeable advice on the rapidly changing world of telecommunications.

Dial-up connections only function while the line is live. Over the horizon are domestic versions of very fast, permanently 'on' connections to the Internet, providing the home user with the same level of access as someone working for an organization. These could be provided either by **ADSL** (asymmetric digital subscriber line), which works over ordinary telephone lines, or **cable modems,** which work on the optical fibre networks of local cable companies. At the time of writing both of these technologies are being tested and are not generally available.

A final option is to use a **cybercafé**, where drop-in Internet access is paid for usually by the hour. The *Internet Café Guide* will show you your nearest cybercafé.

Password security

Whatever your level of Internet access, you will possess a **user identifier** and a **password**, which together identify you to the computer system that you use to access the Internet. Your user identifier is not secret, but your password is. Try not to write your password down in an obvious place (eg on a Post-It note by your computer screen). Your password should not be a word that is locatable in any sort of dictionary, nor should it be traceable to you (eg your car number plate). A good method of arriving at a password is to choose a phrase from a book and derive your password from its initial letters and page number (eg the phrase 'Is this a dagger I see before me' from page 73 of your copy of *Macbeth* gives a password of itadisbm73). You should change your password regularly (as you come across memorable phrases in your reading!).

Site addressing – host and domain names

People and resources on a network have to have a 'site', which is defined in terms of an address of a computer on the network. Thus people are located by the particular computer they use, and information resources by the computer on which they are stored. On the Internet, computer names are made up of two parts, a **host name** and a **domain name**. A domain name is similar to the STD or area code in a telephone number. It tells you where the computer is, and what organization owns it. A host name is an identifying name for a computer within a domain, just as a telephone number identifies an individual in a particular area. Here are some typical examples:

www.ukoln.ac.uk
www.bbc.co.uk
jaffle.lmu.ac.uk

Domain names are normally in three or four parts. Reading right to left, the right-hand part identifies the country of the domain. Most countries have a two-letter country code: **uk** for the United Kingdom, **de** for Germany etc. If there is no country code then the United States is implied, although there is a **us** code which is occasionally seen.

To the left of the country code is a code showing organization type. In the UK domain these are:

ac   for academic
co   for private company
gov   for government
org   for non-profit-making organizations.

In domains for other countries, organization-type codes may vary. For example, domains in the United States and Australia use **edu** for an academic organization, while in most European countries **ac** is used. To understand the organization type in a domain name, a little judgement is called for!

To the left of the organization type is an abbreviated name for an organization. Thus Leeds Metropolitan University is abbreviated to **lmu** and the University of Bath to **bath**. Some organizations are recognizable, others are not.

The host name is the final element. It can be something mundane (like **hp3** for the third Hewlett Packard minicomputer) or it can be something more memorable (like **sloth**).

There are exceptions to these conventions, such as:

portico.bl.uk
pipex.net

In both the above, there is no organization-type code.

Host and domain names together identify a computer on the Internet. An alternative form of computer name which can be used is the **IP address**. This is a string of four numbers separated by full stops (eg **138.38.32.45** for *UKOLN*). These numbers are used in the actual addressing done on the Internet and an automatic translation is done (invisibly to the user) of host and domain names into numbers, by a system known as the **Domain Name System** (DNS).

Domain names can be valuable commodities. Companies are usually very concerned to get a domain name which either matches their company name or is appropriate for their service/products. Originally domain names were issued by *Network Solutions*, Inc and in the UK by *Nominet*, but recently the responsibility for controlling the DNS system (and possibly expanding it by adding new domain 'root' names) has been transferred to a non-profit organization called *ICANN*.

Why are host and domain names important?

The Internet can be difficult to use and understand primarily because the resources it contains have no physical presence for a user, other than on a computer screen. Host and domain names not only locate people and resources but can help the user to infer something more about new resources as they are discovered. Thus a UK television schedule provided by **www.bbc.co.uk** (the BBC) ought to have more authority than one provided on **sloth.cs.du.edu**, a computer (host name **sloth**) located at the Department of Computer Studies at Denver University in the United States (a hypothetical example). This is a guiding principle, not a universal rule; there are some good sources of UK information located on computers in other countries.

See Part 3, Tips on networking problems (p 49) for more information.

PART 2
What is available on the Internet?

Contents

Introduction to Part 2

Fundamentally, the Internet provides access to **people** and to **information resources**. In Part 2 key Internet facilities are looked under these two broad headings. The intention is to help new users understand Internet facilities: hence the major features, advantages and disadvantages of each are described as they affect Internet users generally and LIS professionals in particular. In Part 3 the focus is more practically on effective use of facilities. Many resources are mentioned in Parts 2 and 3. These are cited in italics and they are all described in more detail in Part 4.

Chapter 3
CONTACTING PEOPLE

In this chapter the topic is how to contact people on the Internet. Further details of the resources that are mentioned (in italics) can be found in the Resource Guide in the section on discussion lists and electronic conferences (p81).

People – who are they . . . ?

It is virtually impossible to monitor how many people have Internet access. Some potential users never actually use their Internet connection. Other people have a number of different Internet connections. However, estimates suggest that just under 200 million people currently have access to the Internet (source: *NUA Internet Surveys*). The turnover of users on some sites (eg at universities, when student cohorts change annually) is large. In the UK (as in most countries outside the USA) the majority of users in the early days of the Internet were members of the academic community, but the mid-1990s saw a massive number of non-academic institutions join the Internet, following the trend in the USA where the Internet has for several years been widely used by people in industry, commerce, government and by private citizens.

. . . and how do you contact them?

Essentially there are three ways of communicating with other Internet users: **electronic mail (e-mail), electronic conferencing systems**, and 'live' **interactive systems** where the participants are connected simultaneously. Electronic mail is used by individuals or groups to pass messages between each other and is available to virtually the whole Internet community. Conferencing systems allow people to contribute to a central pool of discussion on a topic; others can then selectively pick up and respond to individual messages in the pool. Live, interactive systems are used to communicate in 'real time'; in effect, participants are 'talking' rather than passing messages between one another.

Electronic mail (e-mail)

E-mail provides a fast, cheap and convenient means of passing messages between individuals and groups. For many users it is the first Internet application they come into contact with and remains the most important.

E-mail addresses

On the Internet, an **e-mail address** is generally made up of three elements:

a user identifier
a separator character – @
a site name.

Thus examples would be:

J.X.Smith@lmu.ac.uk
janet-liaison-desk@jnt.ac.uk

Incoming messages go into a file called a **mailbox** on the computer identified by the host and site name. Usually a user has their own personal mailbox, although it is possible to have a shared mailbox with other users (sales and customer support departments often do this, as in the JANET example above). A **user identifier** can be any combination of letters and numbers: it is obviously useful to have a user identifier related to your name (eg initials followed by surname). Some sites with many users avoid name clashes by adding numbers to the user identifier (eg Jane Smith is J.Smith1, John Smith is J.Smith2, etc).

Receiving e-mail

E-mail appears to the recipient as a list of messages from their mailbox presented by an **e-mailer** (client software for handling e-mail). The display of the messages is determined by the e-mailer you use. There are a range of clients available, and some are included in other packages.

The elements of a typical e-mail include at least:

the sender's name (and/or their e-mail address)
a subject
the date and time sent
the actual message

The **order of messages** is controlled by the e-mailer. The user can usually specify whether messages are ordered by date of arrival, subject, name of sender or message size. All e-mailers allow messages to be read on screen, and printed if necessary. When you read an e-mail message you will see at the top a **header**. This consists of the sender and recipient's e-mail addresses, the subject, the date and time of sending and routing information. The message itself follows the header. Some e-mailers have primitive facilities for searching for a particular message (eg by subject word), or for searching within a message for a word.

All e-mailers allow you to delete messages or to save them in **folders**. A folder is a file of e-mail just like your mailbox, but which you can name in a meaningful way, to enable you to find the e-mail again later. Your e-mailer will allow you to switch to one of these folders to read stored e-mail.

When you exit your e-mailer, it may offer to store all undeleted or unsaved messages in a **received folder**. This will clear your incoming mailbox so that only new messages will appear next time you use it. It is good practice to clear your mailbox each time you use it, although moving it to a received folder can consume an inordinate amount of disk storage space.

See Part 3, Tips on receiving e-mail (p49), for more information.

Sending e-mail

Sending e-mail involves using your e-mailer to enter the e-mail address of the recipient, a subject (short but descriptive) for the e-mail and last, the actual text of the message. Your e-mailer may store all outgoing messages in an outgoing folder. You can use this folder to review past messages you have sent. It is a good idea, when starting out with e-mail, to practise by sending messages to yourself.

Some people end their e-mail messages with a **signature**, a few lines that say who they are, where they work and give contact information like telephone and fax numbers, as well as their e-mail address. Sometimes signatures contain a witty quote or even a graphic, constructed out of characters on the keyboard. While such personalization is encouraged, overlong or controversial signatures can provoke adverse comment. E-mailers can be configured to add a signature to e-mail messages automatically. You may need to create the signature in a separate file first. Note that formatting (italics, bold, etc) is not universally supported in e-mail systems.

Your e-mailer will have a facility to **reply** to a received message. Your reply is usually more meaningful if you add your comments to the text of the original message. You can also **forward** an e-mail message to another person. E-mail messages that you send, reply to or forward can be **copied** so that a number of people are sent the same message.

See Part 3, Tips on sending e-mail (p50), for more information.

Mailing or discussion lists

As well as sending e-mail to individuals, it is also possible to send e-mail to a software program, the most common instance of which is the **mail server**. This is a piece of software which stores a **mailing list** of e-mail addresses of individuals. It can then copy a message from one of those individuals to all the other individuals on the list. Thousands of lists have been set up on the Internet, each devoted to a particular topic, and intended for people who share a common interest to seek, disseminate and share information. In this book we generally use the term **discussion list**, which reflects the participative nature of most lists.

Listserv is a widely used mail server program. It originated in the USA and is now used at sites throughout the world by people who have set up discussion lists on their local Internet host computer. In contrast, the *Mailbase* mail server is popular in the UK and runs many discussion lists from a single site (at the University of Newcastle upon Tyne).

Within librarianship and information science, discussion lists exist that focus on particular professional or research specialisms (eg government documents, collection development, information retrieval). Others bring together people who work in a particular type of library (eg map, music or law), who use a particular type of system or software (eg CD-ROM networks or personal bibliographic software) or who belong to the same professional organization (eg the Institute of Information Scientists). Still others have a geographic focus (eg library automation in Greece) or are intended for people with a similar job or status (eg students, educators).

In the Resource Guide, the section on discussion lists and electronic conferences (p81) contains a few general-purpose library lists and some useful directories. Of particular note is Stephanie da Silva's (*PAML*): *Publicly Accessible Mailing Lists*, which incorporates hobbyist offerings as well as lists with a more serious purpose. *TILE.NET* provides a complete index of Listserv lists. Diane Kovacs and her team at Kent State University Libraries in the USA produce a multidisciplinary *Directory of Scholarly and Professional E-Conferences*, which contains a section on librarianship. The Washington Research Library Consortium compiles a specialist directory of *Library-Oriented Lists and Electronic Serials*, and there is a section devoted to library lists on the *Mailbase Mailing List Service*.

James Milles's *Discussion lists: mailing list manager commands* provides full instructions for joining and using mailing lists on Listserv, *Mailbase* and three other popular mail servers (**Majordomo**, **Listproc** and **Mailserv**). This can be requested by e-mail, as indicated in the Resource Guide. Joining a list is usually a simple matter which just involves sending a standard e-mail message to the address of the mail server (**mailserver@site-name**) leaving the subject line blank. When you join a list you will receive a standard welcome message by e-mail, containing further instructions such as how to contribute messages and to unsubscribe. It is advisable to keep this in a folder for future reference.

In theory, there is no limit to the number of discussion lists you can join. Some discussion lists are **moderated**, which means that there is a person who vets **postings** (messages sent to the discussion list) to ensure their appropriateness, and who may only admit individuals who are truly interested in or knowledgeable about the topic to membership of the list. Since being a moderator involves a lot of work, most discussion lists are unmoderated, and these may carry trivial, erroneous or inflammatory postings as well as messages that do fulfil the purposes of the list. Very few discussion lists actually charge for membership.

When you join a discussion list, you will find that postings come with subject lines attached. Replies or further discussion will use the same subject line, usually preceded by 'Re:'. Replies to your postings may take a while to come in. Many messages never generate any replies, whilst others may start intense debate. When you reply to a posting, include some of the text of the original message. It is not necessary to include all of it, but just enough so that someone who did not see the original posting can follow the debate.

Not all discussion lists allow subscribers to post messages. Some function solely as sources of announcements. Here the term **mailing list** is used for these, for example *New-list* and *New-lists*, which notify subscribers of new Listserv and *Mailbase* lists respectively.

See Part 3, Tips on discussion lists (p53), for more information.

Netiquette

Misunderstandings of meaning are possible with e-mail, and as a consequence informal rules of **netiquette,** of how to conduct an e-mail conversation, have evolved. When sending e-mail to an individual, try to make the meaning of the text of your message as clear as possible. E-mail is a form of communication which is much less formal than traditional paper mail, but which does not carry any clues as to emotional undertones, as, say, listening to a person's voice in a telephone conversation would. The basic rule is to assume nothing about the recipient (in terms of knowledge, emotional state, or general background) unless you have met them and know them well. E-mails have been used in evidence in court cases so do not assume that the seeming informality and impermanence makes them inadmissible. Netiquette is even more important when posting to a discussion list, as you have no idea who may be receiving a message. (See also p54.)

Some discussion lists have little or no message traffic. Not everyone who is a member of a discussion list posts to the list; members who just read postings sent by other people are known as **lurkers**. There is nothing wrong in being a lurker! Discussion lists, just like any social gathering, are dominated by a few people who do most of the 'talking'. Again there is nothing wrong in this; feel free to join in if you have something to say.

The basic rule for posting to a discussion list is to keep your contribution to the topic of the list. Unmoderated discussion lists, however, are particularly prone to off-topic messages and also to **flames** – messages which are phrased in a heated and sometimes abusive manner. Unless you enjoy public argument, avoid sending flames and thus getting involved in '**flame wars**'.

Disadvantages of e-mail

The classic problem of using e-mail is **overload**. Initially you will get few messages, except from your immediate contacts. Then, as you join discussion lists, your mailbox will start to contain more and more new e-mail. It is impossible to quantify overload. Some individuals despair with more than ten messages to read; others can deal happily with hundreds. It is important to structure your day to read e-mail efficiently. A session first thing in the morning will tackle e-mail sent the previous afternoon from people in the United States. Another session at the end of the working day will deal with messages sent that day by people closer to home. Be warned that some people deal with overload by never reading or replying to e-mail! Sometimes individuals post advertisements or inane messages to all the discussion lists or e-mail addresses they can find, whether appropriate or not. This is known as **spamming**. Receiving this sort of e-mail can be extremely annoying.

Another problem of e-mail is its intrinsic lack of **privacy**. Typically, e-mail messages are just text and can be read (albeit with great difficulty) as they are routed from the sender to the recipient via a chain of computers on the Internet. Moreover, the recipient of your e-mail message could forward it to someone you had not intended to receive it. It is never wise to send sensitive information by e-mail. Also e-mail messages can be **faked**. It is prudent to be suspicious about the content of doubtful messages and the identity of senders.

Although e-mail messages are not generally restricted by length, being anything from a word or two to a long discourse, it is difficult to send diagrams or pictures by e-mail. A standard exists, **MIME** (multipurpose Internet mail extension), which your e-mailer may support, for sending all forms of non-textual material via Internet e-mail. However, the recipient's e-mailer may not support MIME, so then there is still a problem.

Finally, another problem of e-mail is not being able to find the e-mail address for a person you want to e-mail. There is no one comprehensive global listing of individual e-mail addresses, basically because such a listing would be enormous, subject to constant flux and difficult to make profitable. E-mail directory services or **white page servers** do exist, but their coverage is very patchy. More often than not they do not contain the person you are looking for. It is often easiest to telephone or write to the person you want to e-mail and ask them what their e-mail address is.

Advantages of e-mail

So, with these disadvantages, why use e-mail? There are a number of convincing reasons. It can cross the globe in minutes. It is free for almost all users, even for those using commercial access providers. Perhaps most important of all is the connection with people that e-mail brings. Questions that cannot be answered by any reference source can be asked on an appropriate discussion list and often bring a flood of responses. While this facility does not work fast enough to be of use at a library reference desk, it is nevertheless impressive. E-mail brings experts from all over the world into your reach. And more than answering the occasional question, membership of a good discussion list brings up-to-the minute news, views, and even gossip on a topic that interests you. There is no substitute in other media for this. Serials, even when produced daily, are behind the times. Radio and television have neither the focus nor depth an expert or an aficionado needs. No other medium allows the level of interaction with other people that e-mail gives.

Electronic conferencing (USENET)

The second way to communicate with people on the Internet is to use **USENET** (also known as **Netnews**), which is a global **conferencing system**. A conferencing system is similar in purpose to a discussion list, in that each **conference** (or **newsgroup**, in USENET terminology) is based on a particular topic. It differs in that readers of a newsgroup read a common pool of messages which make up that newsgroup, rather than receiving individual copies of each message in their own mailbox.

USENET newsgroups

There are currently around 25,000 newsgroups. Newsgroups are organized into categories, the most important of which are:

Category	Topic
bionet	biology
biz	business
comp	anything to do with computers
rec	games, sports and hobbies
misc	topics that don't fit anywhere else
sci	the physical sciences
soc	the culture of countries or social groups

talk	debates on controversial topics
news	topics on USENET itself
alt	'alternative' topics

The precise topic of a newsgroup is indicated by a hierarchical name, which starts with a category, eg:

Newsgroup	*Topic*
comp.mail.elm	the ELM e-mailer
rec.arts.books	novels
sci.maths	mathematics
soc.culture.iran	Iran

TILE.NET provides a complete listing of all USENET newsgroups, including a short description of each one. Newsgroups are also included in the Kovacs *Directory of Scholarly and Professional E-Conferences*. Like discussion lists, some newsgroups are moderated, which means that postings are screened before appearing. Most newsgroups are not moderated. This can lead to extremely bizarre and/or offensive postings (especially in the 'alt' newsgroups).

Articles and threads

Each newsgroup contains one or more **articles** (messages). Articles in USENET newsgroups look very much like e-mail postings. Like e-mail messages, they all have the name of the person posting them and a subject. Each article has a unique identifying number. Some articles are replies to earlier articles. An article and its replies are collectively known as a **thread**. Articles in the same thread all have the same subject header.

Newsreaders

To access USENET you need a **newsreader client**. Just as with e-mailers, there are a number of different clients, available either as separate programs or included with other applications. Which you use is a matter of availability and personal preference.

All newsreaders operate on three levels. The first level is to display a list of **subscribed to** newsgroups, i.e newsgroups you have chosen to read, together with the number of articles (and possibly threads) they contain.

Your newsreader will allow you to move between newsgroups and choose one to read. It will also allow you to see newsgroups that you have not subscribed to and to subscribe to any of them. You will also be able to **unsubscribe from** (ie leave) newsgroups.

Selecting a newsgroup moves you to the second level of newsreader operation, which shows the articles/threads in the newsgroup.

A good newsreader will show only threads and the number of articles they contain. Each thread has a subject and the name of the person who submitted the first article. A poor newsreader will show only articles. You will have to reconstruct threads by looking for similar subjects among the articles. This is a chore.

The last level of newsreader operation is the display of articles/threads themselves. If your newsreader allows you to select a thread, you will then see the first article of the thread. You will be able to read the rest of that article (if it does not fit on the screen) or move on to the next article in the thread. A more limited newsreader will not show threads, only articles, making it hard to follow discussions.

Reading USENET

When you have finished reading articles which interest you in a particular newsgroup, it is wise to use your newsreader to **mark as read** all articles in that newsgroup. This clears out the newsgroup and means that next time you read it, only articles posted after your last reading session will be shown. Your newsreader records what you have read in a small data file (usually called **newsrc** or **.newsrc**, depending on your computer's file-naming conventions). This lists the newsgroups you have subscribed to and the identifying number of the last article you read in each of those newsgroups.

USENET versus e-mail discussion lists

This may all seems very cumbersome, but it is actually easier to read USENET than discussion lists. In your mailbox, messages from different discussion lists are intermixed. Replies to one of your messages may be interspersed throughout your mailbox with messages on other subjects. In contrast, each newsgroup is self-contained. A threaded newsreader can compress many articles into threads and show you on one screen the total activity of a newsgroup. It is possible to read certain discussion lists as USENET groups. These are found in the **bit.listserv** hierarchy. Discussion lists on librarianship topics that can be read as newsgroups can be located via Washington Research Library Consortium's *Library-Oriented Lists and Electronic Serials*.

For the newcomer, though, USENET can be daunting. With e-mail you start with an empty mailbox. With USENET you may start automatically subscribed to hundreds of newsgroups. The best thing to do is to unsubscribe to all groups, except the couple intended for new users:

news.announce.newusers
news.newusers.questions

When you have mastered reading these, then start looking for more interesting newsgroups.

See Part 3, Tips on reading USENET newsgroups (p55), for more information.

Posting messages to USENET

Where does the pool of messages that form USENET come from? Your newsreader will enable you to **post** a message to a particular newsgroup. This message is then relayed to neighbouring sites which take their **newsfeed** from your site. These sites will pass on your message and eventually it will reach every site which takes USENET. Incoming messages reach your site in a similar manner, being passed along a chain of newsfeed sites.

Before you post to a newsgroup, be sure you have read the **FAQ** (frequently asked questions) document published by many newsgroups. This document is a compendium of the newsgroup's wisdom and should answer obvious questions that might be asked about the topic of the newsgroup. FAQs are normally posted on a regular basis to a newsgroup, at least once a month. For the seeker of information, a FAQ can be invaluable. There is a USENET group which publishes nothing but FAQs, called **news.answers**. *Network News* at the University of Oxford provides a major repository of newsgroup FAQs.

It is also imperative to follow netiquette when posting to newsgroups, just as when posting to discussion lists.

See Part 3, Tips on posting to USENET newsgroups (p57), for more information.

Access to USENET

Not all sites have a host machine for storing USENET newsgroups and those that do may not take all newsgroups. There are a number of reasons for this. The volume of articles added daily to USENET is immense and requires a lot of central disk-storage at a site. As a result, articles are **expired** after a set period (which varies between sites) and deleted to save storage space. If you read USENET you must read it regularly or you will miss things! Some newsgroups are intended for an audience within a defined geographical region. Newsgroups in the **uk** category, for example, concern UK-related issues and thus are not likely to be taken at a non-UK site. A few newsgroups have to be paid for, notably the **clari** category, which carries copyrighted news stories supplied by Associated Press and Reuters.

Perhaps the main reason why not all newsgroups are taken by many sites is concern over their content. Many newsgroups in the **alt** category are conduits of all sorts of strange and sometimes unpleasant postings. The **alt.sex** hierarchy has been widely banned because of worries over its explicit pornographic content. Newsgroups like **alt.flame** exist only to provoke heated argument. But, just as it is unfair to judge a newsagent's only by its top shelf, USENET contains many stimulating, erudite newsgroups. The advantages of USENET, then, are very similar to those of e-mail. If the name of a newsgroup does not sound inviting, and a glance at its contents reveals nothing of interest, then move on and look elsewhere.

Interactive systems

Internet relay chat (IRC)

Whereas e-mail and USENET are (on the whole) **asynchronous** – in other words, there is normally a time lag between messages being sent and read – some systems allow conversations to be held live and are said to be **synchronous**. Participants have to be simultaneously online but can interact. One example is **Internet relay chat** (**IRC**) where messages can be typed and received almost simultaneously between users around the world.

Special client software is needed to access IRC. IRC allows you to join a **channel** – a discussion. Channels can be public or private (open to only a few people). Individuals on IRC channels tend to be known by adopted **nicknames**. Using IRC you can list channels, and join and leave channels. Once you have joined a channel, anything you type is echoed (copied) to the screens of the other users on that channel, following your nickname. You can list the current individuals on a channel and message them individually if you want.

Conversations on IRC tend to be gossipy. Some sites consider IRC to be nothing but a time-waster and do not allow its use. Occasionally, though, IRC can have real importance when news events are reported live by eye witnesses via IRC news channels.

Instant messaging

Chat forms a continuous stream. An **instant messaging** facility enables you to find out if people you want to communicate with are online and then send them messages, and vice versa. Thus messaging is not always continuous, but potentially could be. Most instant messaging systems are adding voice (in the form of sound files) and can also set up chat connections. The leading software package for instant messaging is *ICQ*, which is meant to stand for 'I seek you'.

Internet telephony and videoconferencing

Internet telephony involves using the Internet as an intermediary between ordinary telephone systems. A 'call' is made from a computer using special software and a microphone and is then routed through the Internet until it emerges at a junction with the local telephone system on which the intended recipient of the call has their standard telephone connection. It is useful for saving money on international calls, as only local calls are chargeable either end.

Videoconferencing works in a similar manner, except that the connection never leaves the Internet. Both originator and recipient need a special video camera, whose output is sent via a fast Internet connection to the other. The main problem is not the cost of the video cameras but in the high speed of the Internet connection required for decent picture and sound quality at either end. Since the speed of a connection cannot be guaranteed across the public Internet, videoconferencing across it is still a hit-and-miss affair.

MUDS and MOOS

Similar to IRC in that participants are connected in real time, but different in that an imaginary 'locale' is added to contextualize interactions, is a **MUD (multi-user dungeon)**. The first MUD was a role-playing fantasy game in which participants pretended to be elves, dwarves etc. The MUD would give them a textual description of their character's viewpoint and show them the results of their commands (actions in the MUD). Knowledgeable participants, known as **wizards**, could change or add features to the computer-generated setting. There are now a host of different types of MUD, classified by the capabilities of the software which generates the setting and handles interactions. The latest generation, using up-to-date software techniques, goes by the name of **MOO (MUD object-oriented)**.

MUDs and their ilk can be extremely enjoyable (if you like role-playing games). However, dedicated players have been known to play them to the exclusion of all else. Some sites forbid their use on the same grounds as IRC. MUDs are chiefly textual, but a new generation of graphical MUDs is appearing (for example Worldsaway, from CompuServe). Apart from playing games, MUDs and MOOs can be used for educational purposes (holding tutorials for distant participants) and **live conferencing**. The Kovacs *Directory of Scholarly and Professional E-Conferences* now includes MUDs and MOOs that have a scholarly or pedagogical rationale.

Chapter 4
ACCESSING INFORMATION RESOURCES

Information resources – what are they . . . ?

Information resources on the Internet are all stored as **computer files** of some kind. They have a location on at least one Internet site, but may be duplicated at other (**mirror**) sites. Each file has a **filename** (according to the conventions of the computer where it is located) and a **pathname** which defines the **directory** and **subdirectories** in which it is stored, starting from a **root** (initial) directory at its own site.

Typically, a file entitled 'handbook' in the 'guides' subdirectory of the 'training' directory in the root directory of a particular site would have a pathname:

/training/guides/handbook

Computer files on the Internet contain materials as varied as the text of the King James Bible, images of the Beowulf manuscript, the opening speech from the original Star Trek series, videos of NASA space missions and up-to-the-minute news headlines from CNN.

In this chapter, it is first necessary to consider how to access the files and then second to identify types of text and software files that are likely to be of interest to the library and information professions generally. Further details of specific resources which are named (in italics in the text) can be found in the sections in Part 4 on resources linked to Part 2.

. . . and how do you access them?

A number of different means of accessing files have evolved along with the Internet. All involve the use of a special client package, which can either operate alone or as part of some other package.

The basic means of access to files at a remote site is a **telnet** client. Telnet opens a live link between your computer and an information server or gateway on the Internet, identified by a host and domain name. To use telnet you need to have a valid user id and password for the remote site.

See Part 3, Tips on using telnet (p58), for more information.

To avoid problems of user authentication, some sites in the early days of the Internet set themselves up as **bulletin board systems (BBS)**, which allowed users to login as guests, without passwords. Once logged in, users could browse files.

Another way of avoiding user authentication is **anonymous file transfer,** using the **file transfer protocol (FTP)**. Sites would set up special directories of files that allowed remote users to login as 'anonymous', giving their e-mail address as a password. FTP became very popular, so much so that so many sites started offering so many files that a search service, *Archie*, was set up to allow users to search for a file by name and find out at which sites it was stored. To minimize network traffic, special sites called **mirrors** were set up by region or country, to hold copies of popular collections of files from sites around the world. The main UK mirror is SunSITE, at Imperial College, London.

See Part 3, Tips on using FTP (p59), for more information.

For many years BBS and FTP were the only means of accessing files. In the early 1990s the University of Minnesota released a package called **Gopher**. The gopher, the state animal of Minnesota, is a small rodent which burrows its way to food. Thus Gopher 'burrowed' to files on the Internet. It offered a series of menus which the user navigated to get to a link to the file they wanted. For its time Gopher was revolutionary. It made knowing where a file was stored no longer important, removing an enormous burden from users. However, the menu display was relatively inflexible, and unexciting. Gopher was swept away in 1993 by a new means of file retrieval, which allowed a flexible and colourful display of links to files to be accessible by a simple click of the mouse.

World wide web

The world wide web began as a **hypertext** publishing project for research papers over a local network at CERN (European Organization for Nuclear Research) in Geneva. Its success at CERN soon saw it applied to files on the Internet. Hypertext is linked text: a highlighted word or phrase in one piece of text, when activated, leads to a different piece of text related to the chosen word or phrase.

Hypertext browsing is not without problems, but it offered a number of advantages over Gopher's somewhat restrictive menu structures. World wide web links could be embedded in text anywhere on a **page**, ie a text file marked up in a language called **HTML (hypertext markup language)**. HTML, a derivative of **SGML (standard generalized markup language)**, allowed the formatting of a page to be controlled by means of **tags**, which indicate the nature of particular page **elements** (title, headings, paragraphs, lists etc). It was possible to embed graphics in pages, making them better looking than text-only Gopher menus.

A link to another page or resource is expressed by a **URL (uniform resource** locator), which gives the retrieval method (usually **http,** the **hypertext transfer protocol** for the web), the host and domain name, and the path and file name of the page to be retrieved. For example, the URL for the *Internet Resources Newsletter* is:

http://www.hw.ac.uk/libWWW/irn/irn/html

where:

http	is the retrieval method
www.hw.ac.uk	is the host and domain name (Heriot-Watt University, UK)
libWWW/irn/irn.html	is the path and filename (the irn.html file in the **libWWW/irn** directory).

URLs can point to resources under a variety of Internet tools besides the web (eg FTP, telnet, USENET and Gopher) by replacing **http** in the URL by **ftp, telnet, news** or **gopher** respectively.

The web really took off in early 1993 when the University of Illinois at Urbana-Champaign made freely available for non-commercial use a **browser** (ie a web client) called **Mosaic**, which ran under popular graphical user interfaces like Microsoft Windows, Macintosh and X-Windows. Mosaic became the 'acceptable face of the Internet', and rapidly began to attract commercial interest. The development team of Mosaic left to start their own company, and produced an even more popular browser, *Netscape*. Mosaic itself attracted commercial licensing deals and many software houses are developing their own web browsers. Microsoft has produced a rival to *Netscape*, **Internet Explorer**.

On startup, all browsers display a user-definable **home page**, which may be set up by your Internet access provider. You can then click on the links provided, or open a link to any other URL you specify. The links you follow are recorded in a **history list**, and there are simple forward and back facilities to enable you to retrace your path. All browsers support a **hotlist** or **bookmark** facility, whereby you can record the URLs of interesting pages for future reference. Some browsers allow bookmarks to be configured hierarchically, to allow the structured storage of URLs for interesting pages.

On the server side, it is easy for people to publish information themselves, as HTML is reasonably straightforward, and software tools for HTML markup are readily available. Creating personal **home pages** got many people interested in publishing information on the Internet.

As the web grew, it developed in two ways. One way has been the accretion of new or co-opted technologies that have been incorporated into the web. URLs could be used to retrieve and deliver sound and video by means of **plug-ins** (extra software modules in a browser which act on a specific file type) and **helpers** (external software that can be automatically run by a browser). Early on, sound and video files had to be downloaded in their entirety before they could be viewed. Later **web cams**, static cameras trained on a view of a place, etc, appeared, and these led in turn to a way of delivering radio and television content over the Internet. **Streaming** is the sending of a continuous flow of data, typically sound or video, formatted in such a way as to preserve as much quality as possible across the Internet. Television channels appear in postage-stamp sized windows and radio stations can now broadcast globally for the cost of an Internet connection.

Standard web pages consisting of HTML coding are static: they only have one appearance/function. Including program code in pages can make them dynamic, ie change in response to input from a user, and can greatly extend their function-ality. **Javascript** is a programming language developed especially for use in web pages. Its big brother is **Java**, a revolutionary programming language which can provide the same functionality on any computer system that can run a browser. These are known as client-side programming languages, in that they run in a user's browser and not on a remote server. Using these languages, it is possible to deliver just about any computer application via the web, leading to the concept of the **network computer**, a computer which in itself is devoid of storage and func-tion, but can be activated by software etc from the web.

See Part 3, Tips on using the web (p61), for more information.

Subject listings and search engines

The other way the web developed was in sheer size. Nobody knows for sure how many web pages there are. Estimates currently range from 800 million up. Thus, following links on web pages can take you on an endless path. The practice of exploring links to see where they lead, is known as **surfing** and can be fun. However, for the serious information seeker, better ways of finding useful pages are needed. Subject listings and search engines are the two main ways to locate information.

Subject listings tend to organize Internet resources under broad subject headings. These listings are also sometimes called directories, virtual libraries or subject gateways but all are generally characterized by the input of human effort into creating these listings. Another important characteristic is that subject listings generally have structure. In addition to keyword searching you can navigate this structure and scan the information contained without needing any particular pic-ture of what you want to find. Probably the most popular of these directory ser-vices is *Yahoo!* which organizes Internet resources into hierarchical subject listings that can be browsed or searched. In the UK there are a number of subject gateways, such as EEVL, HUMBUL, OMNI and SOSIG. These services were funded initially under the *Electronic Libraries Programme*, and are now part of the UK *Resource Discovery Network*. These gateways are selective services evaluating and describing Internet resources according to strict criteria. The *World Wide Web Virtual Library* is probably the oldest catalogue of the web and is a distributed collection of subject-specific listings maintained by volunteers. Another impressive volunteer effort is the *Open Directory Project* which aims to construct the most comprehensive web directory using the input of several thousand volunteer editors, who select and add resources to the service.

The subject listings services are impressive, but can only be as accurate and comprehensive as the efforts of their compilers allow. This is where services with commercial backing or government sponsorship can score over those maintained by volunteers.

The alternative method creates searchable indexes of words from web pages, typically known as **search engines**. Examples of this type are *Lycos*, *AltaVista*, *Infoseek* and *HotBot*. These massive indexes are created by a software program known as a **spider, robot** or **crawler**, which starts with one web page and follows all the links it contains, then all the subsequent links and so on. Users' search keywords are matched against the indexes using **relevance ranking** techniques, which aim to retrieve and rank the pages that **best match** the user's query and to allocate a numeric score accordingly (how well they do this is sometimes a matter for speculation). Although these indexes are impressive, the rate of growth at which new web servers are appearing makes indexing difficult. There is an ever-increasing amount of material to index, and all of it just uncontrolled text. So whilst search engines can index millions of web pages, it is still estimated that any one search engine only covers 20–30% of the web at best. Because of differing gathering techniques or coverage policies the content of search engines can differ. If you want to undertake a comprehensive search of the web it might be worth using a **meta search engine**: these search across a number of search engines at the same time and present the integrated results to you on a single page (*MetaCrawler* is a good example of this type of service). *SearchEngineWatch* provides an excellent overview of the different capabilities of search engines as well as reviews and tutorials.

See Part 3, Searching the Internet (p63), for more information.

Portals and e-business

Yahoo! has already been mentioned in relation to searching the Internet. However, an examination of Yahoo will reveal that searching is not the only service it offers. There is a range of personalized facilities, like free e-mail, free Internet access, an online calendar/diary and messaging. There are also meeting places, like conferencing areas, chat lines and online games. Finally, there is a strong element of commerce, both in advertising on screen but also in links to online shops, auction rooms and classified advertising. All these elements are built into one simple screen. This mixture is known as a **portal**, as it has been designed simply and solely both to act as a gateway but also to try to hold onto its visitors and if possible make them spend money on something. Certainly the top portals are overwhelmingly the first Internet destination of most Internet users.

Yahoo! is currently by far the most successful single portal, but it is being chased by *AOL* (America Online) and *MSN* (MicroSoft Network). Apart from portals there are a range of e-business servers, which exist to sell a service or a product often in a way not seen off the Internet. Traditional auctions have carried over well onto the Internet. Perhaps the best known of the online auction sites is *eBay*. The mass of people on the Internet make it ideal for auctions which need plenty of buyers and sellers. But some e-business works in ways which seem strange. *Buy.com*, for example, sells goods at cost price and makes profits only from advertisements. *Priceline.com* allows people to bid for whatever product or service they want and then attempts to find a supplier at that price. Where once purely information was the reason for a server, now business is finding and creating a range of new niches for itself on the Internet.

Information servers and gateways

If servers promoting business are new and currently in the spotlight, there are still plenty of excellent information servers and gateways which are publicly funded and providing services that business would never be interested in.

The earliest form of information server was the bulletin board, which provided access to information and information services via a series of menus. The software to do this was typically specially written. Bulletin boards usually focus on a particular subject area (eg the humanities, or library and information studies) or are aimed at certain user groups (eg the members of a particular organization). The first bulletin boards gave access to files stored at one site. Many of the chief information servers and gateways in the UK started off as bulletin boards on JANET, such as The *BUBL Information Service* (originally, the **Bulletin Board for Libraries**) and the *NISS Information Gateway*.

Another early type of bulletin board, intended for **community information**, was the **Freenet**. Freenets are community networks intended to provide free local, cultural, recreational and business information for a particular locality. The first Freenet was in Cleveland, Ohio. They quickly spread throughout North America and there are a few in Europe. A Freenet may present a menu that resembles a main street, with choices for the 'town hall', the 'public library', etc. Freenets are accessible from the Internet (eg via the *Free-Nets and Community*

Networks server), and provide their local communities with limited access to the Internet.

Bulletin boards are usually very easy to use, although it can be tedious going through several menu screens to reach the desired information – especially if what you are looking for is not there after all! There is often no way of anticipating what may be on the next menu screen or of knowing how relevant or complete the information will be when you get to it.

The latest type of information server is known as **web logs**. In themselves they publish nothing new but collect and organize links to the best new information on the web in their chosen field. Usually run by dedicated individuals, they currently provide some of the best information available via the Internet. *Arts and Letters Daily* is especially recommended.

OPACs and library-based information servers

The **online public access catalogues** (OPACs) of over 150 academic and research libraries in the UK – and thousands more in other parts of the world – can be accessed via telnet, Gopher and the web.

Hytelnet provides authoritative listings of what is available throughout the world, while the *CARL Corporation* links to hundreds of public, academic and school libraries in the USA. The *UK Higher Education Library Catalogues* from NISS is the major gateway to UK OPACs.

Unfortunately, if you want to trace bibliographic details of a hard-to-find item, there is no easy way of knowing which OPAC to try, although NISS does attempt to indicate subject strengths of particular OPACs. Coverage of this information is, however, patchy. *COPAC* provides unified access to 15 UK research libraries' online catalogues, with plans to add several more over the next few years.

There are many software platforms for OPACs offered by different commercial library automation suppliers. They each have their own search procedures. Although on-screen help is invariably provided, and basic instructions for searching most of the major systems are available through directories like *Hytelnet*, this situation is far from ideal. Hence many of the first applications of Z39.50 (a protocol for searching one or more different databases simultaneously) were initiated by libraries in the USA to provide an alternative but standard method for searching their bibliographic holdings data and other databases, such as circulation files. So far, few UK libraries have followed suit, though some library system suppliers are offering an option for access via Z39.50 servers.

Academic libraries in the USA have been particularly active in setting up web servers to act as interfaces to their resources and services. Janet Foster's *Innovative Internet Applications in Libraries* is a good place to start investigating the imaginative range of different services which (mostly) US libraries are now offering over the

Internet. Thomas Dowling's *LibWeb* links to library-based web servers worldwide, including a number in Europe and the UK. There is a discussion list, *Web4Lib*, for librarians who are interested in setting up library-based web servers and clients.

In addition, some major national catalogues and bibliographies are available – the Library of Congress catalogue (Locis) is searchable via the *Library of Congress Home Page* (including a Z39.50 facility if you have a Z39.50 client). The British Library's OPAC 97 (available via the *Portico* gateway) is a free service, partially funded by sponsorship from *Amazon.co.uk*, which allows you to find out what material is held in the major reference and document supply collections of the British Library.

Information servers from other organizations

The advent of the web has seen a burgeoning number of information servers being set up by organizations of all types, often to promote the organization and its goods and services. The last sections of the Resource Guide are devoted to organizational servers that will be of general interest to library and information professionals. Of particular note here are catalogues now available from many UK publishers, and a rapidly growing number of bookshops are offering booklists and online ordering to the public at large. Broadcast and news media are offering TV and radio schedules, news summaries and the like. Further information can be found in the Resource Guide under *Booksellers, publishers and the media* (p121).

Many of the commercial online information retrieval services are accessible by telnet or web interfaces, bringing free if not necessarily more reliable telecommunications links to these services for many subscribers. These are listed in a section of the Resource Guide on *Commercial online information retrieval services* (p123).

Also spotlighted in the Resource Guide are government, government-related and international organizations (p119), library and information education (p127), and LIS and related professional associations (p129).

Information resources of interest to the library and information professional

Directories of Internet resources

Directories of discussion lists, software, library OPACs and other Internet resources are plentiful. The Internet has been criticized for its lack of 'meta-resources' but the situation has changed rapidly over recent years. The real problem is that it is impossible for a single directory to cover its field comprehensively. Moreover, it is not always clear to the user how comprehensive or authoritative a directory is, what precisely it aims to include, or how often it is updated. Too many directories that are not kept up to date can still be found on the Internet. We have included directories of Internet resources in each section of the Resource Guide, and have aimed to single out ones that complement each other and that are recognized and authoritative.

Discussion lists and electronic conferences – archives and FAQs

Discussion lists and USENET newsgroups only perform distribution, not storage. However, postings to some discussion lists and newsgroups are archived at a site, and these can be helpful to get a flavour of the group before joining. Sometimes they contain compilations of Internet resources pertinent to the subject of the list. In the UK, the SunSITE gateway provides an archive of USENET newsgroups, while *Deja* has archives of most mainstream newsgroups going back to early 1995. *Network News* at Oxford University is a good source of newsgroup FAQs. Archives for all *Mailbase* lists are available via the *Mailbase Mailing List Service*.

Electronic journals, newsletters and alerting services

Electronic serials reflect the diversity that is found in printed publications – from popular magazines, newsletters and newspapers to scholarly academic journals. There are all sorts of hobbyist offerings, fiction magazines and **zines** (small publications usually produced by an individual and not-for-profit) on the Internet, as well as a wealth of material aimed at the academic and professional user.

Many electronic journals are freely distributed as text files to members of mailing and discussion lists, though occasionally by USENET. Publication and distribution schedules range from the regular to the highly erratic. Archives of back issues may be kept at a particular site.

While electronic journals share many of the characteristics of conventional serial publications, there are differences. Those distributed via e-mail are almost invariably text only, but some commercial and populist offerings are pioneering the inclusion of graphics. Even text-only e-journals can offer 'value added' features over printed publications. For example, *PACS-Review* enables authors to 'revisit' their articles in order to update them. The 'top' articles, according to how often they are visited in an archive, are monitored.

Scholarly electronic journals have editorial boards and subject articles to peer review which is intrinsically no less rigorous than conventional publishing, so the originally rather guarded response from some sectors of the academic community towards the intellectual authority of scholarly e-journals is disappearing. It is not unusual for academics to take on the roles of e-journal editor, reviewer or distributor on a voluntary basis, thus bypassing the conventional publisher altogether.

The advent of electronic journals has revived the early traditions of academic publishing, whereby readers would enter into a correspondence with the original author. This is easy to do electronically, and in this sense the electronic journal blurs the distinction between a publication and a discussion forum.

In contrast to the scholarly e-journal, the Internet offers a wealth of electronic newsletters which tend to more frequent publication and shorter publication schedules for items of topical interest. *Ariadne,* for example, is a prominent newsletter in the fields of library networking and technology. *Current Cites* is an alerting service which covers a similar field, with citations and short abstracts to articles in other printed and electronic journals.

The *Directory of Electronic Journals, Newsletters and Academic Discussion Lists*, produced by the American Association of Research Libraries (ARL), offers one of the most comprehensive, multidisciplinary listings of e-journals. It is available on the Internet and in print format, and includes a section on library and information studies. Washington Research Library Consortium's *Library-Oriented Lists and Electronic Serials*, which was mentioned in the last chapter, offers specialist coverage of LIS. Both of these directories can be requested by electronic mail. You can receive notification of new additions to the ARL directory by subscribing to the *NewJour* mailing list. Details are given in the Resource Guide.

Traditional publishers have finally caught up with the electronic publishing medium and many now offer Internet-based access to their publications. **IngentaJournals** which is the commercial arm of BIDS, offers access to over 150,000 full-text electronic articles from 800 leading academic journals. The **National Electronic Site Licensing Initiative** (NESLI) is a three year *JISC*-funded programme to deliver a national electronic journal service to UK Higher Education.

Full-text archives

Well-established archives of online books and shorter works available on the Internet include the Alex Catalog of Electronic Texts on the Internet, Project Gutenberg and the Oxford Text Archive. These contain the full text of classic works, ranging from translations of ancient Greek and Roman authors to the nineteenth century novel, and covering subjects from politics to religion, history to philosophy. Normally, these are collections of out-of-copyright material which are freely available over the Internet, though still subject to some form of copyright restrictions which prevent redistribution. They are not intended as an alternative to curling up on the sofa with a good book, although the perverse may choose to do so! In fact they are aimed at humanities scholars, for the purposes of content, structural and linguistic analysis and would normally be used in conjunction with indexing, concordance or other text analysis software. As such, they represent a specialized interest, and so we have not included them in the Resource Guide, though they can be easily traced via information servers such as *BUBL*.

General reference works

There are some general works of reference to be found on the Internet, notably technical, English and foreign-language dictionaries, thesauri such as Roget's, acronym dictionaries and the like. Some good compilations of reference works from the USA are also included in the Resource Guide. The commercial reality, however, is that publishers simply do not distribute their material for nothing. Some encyclopaedia publishers have made their works available for paying users on commercial services like CompuServe and Prodigy; *Britannica Online* offers a free demonstration service.

Software and multimedia

There are many thousands of software packages available on the Internet, both **shareware** (which allows free trial use) and **freeware,** for all purposes and all makes of computer. Obviously you will not find mainstream commercial packages. However, documentation for commercial packages can sometimes be found, as well as much discussion and information-exchange from user-groups. Networking and general utility software, however, is available in abundance, including a wealth of client and server programs for accessing and setting up Internet applications, and utilities for computer systems support supplied by everyone from enthusiasts to major software companies like Microsoft (on the *EMWAC* server). There are also many specialist applications packages for particular subjects, including librarianship.

Software archives are held at a number of sites on the Internet. For UK users in higher education, *the UK Mirror Service* is probably the major source, while *Shareware.com* acts as a composite site for searching materials in 20 other managed archives. Software can also be located at some of the sites listed in the Resource Guide under 'Networking organizations', notably the huge, multidisciplinary *Archive: SunSITE Northern Europe* at Imperial College, London. Although these sites take reasonable precautions, it is always wise to virus-check any software you obtain from an archive before running it.

As well as software there are now impressive collections of images, sound and video. A good guide to these is *Digital Librarian: Audio, Video, Rich Media.* There are also search engines specializing in finding multimedia. See the Subject listings and search engines resource section (p88), for more information.

Networking guides and training materials

There is a plethora of free documents and training materials which are intended for all Internet applications and all types and levels of user. Like selecting a book from a publisher's catalogue, it is not always obvious which to choose, so a few have been picked out for the Resource Guide that give a clear explanation of a range of Internet tools (p114), though there are many more that could be recommended.

Cataloguing, evaluation and citing of Internet resources

Traditionally libraries have created bibliographic records for only the materials that they physically hold in their collections; however, user demands for access to Internet resources has required libraries to step outside of this traditional role and to begin to provide this access. There are two main approaches to cataloguing Internet resources:

* Using traditional cataloguing practices such as MARC and AACR2 to create bibliographic records of Internet resources to fit into a library OPAC. OCLC's CORC Project is a good example of this method. It uses the traditional cooperative cataloguing model to create MARC records for Internet resources.
* Cataloguing Internet resources using simple **metadata** formats. Metadata is structured data about data that is used to describe Internet resources. Subject gateways are a good example of this approach, involving the expertise of librarians to select and describe Internet resources using metadata.

There are pros and cons to both approaches. However, library cataloguing formats such as MARC are complex processes developed to describe print materials, which tend to be static in nature. Unlike printed materials Internet resources are far from static: they grow and change on a regular basis or sometimes disappear altogether without warning. Metadata formats such as the **Dublin Core** have been developed specifically to describe electronic sources of information and as such are more lightweight and adaptable to these changes. The Dublin Core is a set of 15 elements (or fields) that has been developed by the library and networking community to provide an international standard for describing Internet resources. The *IFLANET* site has a good overview section on cataloguing and indexing electronic resources.

Evaluating Internet resources

Whatever the approach it is important that librarians get involved in cataloguing and organizing Internet resources, as they have the core skills required not only to catalogue but also to evaluate and select resources. In an environment where anyone can publish anything, the evaluative skills of librarians are vital to guide their users to information that is valid, authoritative and accurate. Being aware of the potential pitfalls of material found on the Internet will be a necessary requirement for anyone using the web to gather information. Asking who is providing the information, and why, is a fundamental question that needs to be asked of all information found on the Internet. The *Internet Detective* is an interactive online tutorial which provides a useful overview of the need to evaluate Internet information as well as quizzes and worked examples to enforce the learning process.

Citing Internet resources

There is no one standard way of citing electronic resources. However *Bibliographic Formats for Citing Electronic Information* makes use of two common citation styles from the Modern Language Association (MLA) and the American Psychological Association (APA).

PART 3
Using the Internet effectively

Contents

Introduction to Part 3

This part contains advice on how to use the Internet effectively. It assumes that Part II has been read or that the reader has a basic knowledge of Internet resources and tools. Unless otherwise noted, resources mentioned in this part appear under 'Utilities' in Part 4 (p133).

Chapter 5
BASIC NETWORKING PROBLEMS, E-MAIL AND USENET

Tips on networking problems

Ever wonder what you can do about messages such as 'server does not have a DNS entry' or 'The server is down or unreachable'? The first thing to do is re-try a couple of times. These network problems can be transient. If that does not work, what do you do?

The first error message is saying that the site you want does not exist. To check this use *Whois*, which is a search facility on the DNS (Domain Name System) itself. It will tell you not only if a site exists, but who owns it, etc. If *Whois* says that site exists, but you get a DNS error trying to access it, then there is a serious network problem. Consult your ISP immediately. If *Whois* does not know about the site you want then you have been given an erroneous site reference.

The second error message denotes something amiss on the network or with the server you are trying to contact. **Traceroute** is a utility which shows you the route that packets take to move from your machine to the server you want to access. This route can reveal slow spots or blockages. It might be, for example, that the server you want to reach is working perfectly but that something between you and it is broken and not working. Running traceroute reveals a numbered list of sites through which your connection travels. Against each site is an access time: asterisks only against a number in the site list reveals a blockage.

It may be that you have a traceroute application already on your machine. If not, then use the *LINX Looking Glass*. The latter is a public service provided by the London Internet Exchange, which acts as a switching service between UK sites and the rest of the Internet.

Tips on receiving e-mail

E-mail tends to accumulate quickly over time. You may find that you exceed your **disk quota** (permitted storage space) on the computer that stores your e-mail. **Mail-bombing** is the unpleasant practice of deliberately sending someone a large amount of e-mail so that their disk quota is exceeded.

It is advisable to delete most of the e-mail you receive, unless you really think you will need to refer to it later. Another way of saving on storage space is to disable (using your e-mailer) your outgoing and received folders. If you want to retain any messages, store them in folders that you name yourself (your e-mailer should allow you to do this). E-mail in suitably named folders is easier to find later, for reference or deletion. Of course, you can always print your e-mail, and then delete it.

If you pay a time-related charge to access the Internet, it ought to be possible to **download** e-mail from your Internet host onto your personal computer. This will enable you to store e-mail locally and delete it from the host computer. You can then read it and reply to messages when not connected to the Internet. Obviously to send a message you must reconnect and then send the replies you have accumulated. E-mailers offering this feature are known as **off-line readers**.

Finally, beware that it is possible to receive a virus in an attachment to an e-mail. The virus is only activated if the attachment is opened. The most common type of virus spread this way is a **macro virus**, so called as it uses the in-built macro language of common software applications, typically those of Microsoft Office. Most virus checkers will guard against this eventuality. You may get warnings that viruses can be spread by just reading an e-mail. This is nonsense. *Urban Legends and Folklore* is an excellent resource debunking this and other Internet myths.

Tips on sending e-mail

Storing addresses

To avoid having to type e-mail addresses for regular correspondents over and over again, your e-mailer should allow you to set up **aliases** (also known as **nicknames**) which link short names (eg Jane) with full e-mail addresses (eg **J.X.Smith@bl.uk**). You only have to enter the short name when addressing e-mail. Your **alias list** functions like an address book for e-mail identifiers. If someone e-mails you first, your e-mailer ought to be able to create an alias from the address details in their message.

Sending attachments

It is possible to send non-text files by e-mail, such as images or word processed documents. Look in your e-mailer for a command to **attach files**. Once you have written your text message you will need to tell the e-mailer where to pick up the file you want to attach: you can do this by browsing through your system and selecting the file.

Confirming receipt

When you have sent an e-mail to someone, how do you know whether it has been received and read? You know that it is in the addressee's incoming mailbox if the message does not **bounce** (ie return to you because of some error, typically an incorrect address). Bounced e-mails will contain a reason for their return.

Unfortunately, it is impossible to know if the e-mail has been read. Confirmation messages indicating an e-mail has been opened typically do not work over the Internet. It may be possible to know if the recipient has logged in after you sent the e-mail. There is a piece of software called **finger**, which takes an e-mail address and tells you when that person last logged in. Note that not all sites allow their users to be 'fingered' from remote sites, as this is seen as a security risk.

If you are worried about the receipt of an urgent e-mail, you can try e-mailing the **postmaster** at a site. The postmaster is the person responsible for managing the e-mail system at a site, and all sites should have one. The postmaster's e-mail address is always **postmaster@***site*.

Finding e-mail addresses

It is usually straightforward to find the e-mail address of someone at your own site. Ask your Internet access provider about local directory services. It can be a bigger problem to find an address for someone at a different site. You are advised to consult the list of services on *WhoWhere*.

Further netiquette

To the basic rules of netiquette one can add many more, which are appropriate in different circumstances. Arlene Rinaldi's *The Net: User Guidelines and Netiquette* is a well-respected guide. Perhaps the only significant point to add to her recommendations is to avoid using culturally specific language. UK colloquialisms or metaphors may not be understood abroad.

All e-mail messages (and USENET postings) have to be formed from the characters on a keyboard. To reduce the time spent keying text, a range of **abbreviations** and **jargon terms** are in common usage. **Newbie**, for example, is a person new and inexperienced in Internet lore. Many abbreviations can be deduced from their context, eg **btw** for 'by the way', **IMO** for 'in my opinion'. The *Jargon File Resources* is an extensive glossary of such abbreviations.

Finally, to try to add a measure of emotional undertone to text messages, **smileys** (also known as **emoticons**) have evolved. Created from keyboard characters, they are to be imagined as a face laid sideways, eg

:-)   is a smiling face (indicating humour)

:-(is a sad face (indicating regret).

There is an *Unofficial Smiley Dictionary* in the EFF's Guide to the Internet.

E-mail privacy, security and anonymity

If you are worried about privacy or security (eg sending sensitive information by e-mail) then use standard **encryption**. Encryption software works by encrypting (transforming) your text into a near-random string of characters, using a **password**. This password is required to get the encryption software to change the encrypted message back into text. Some e-mailers offer encryption facilities.

There are two problems with using built-in e-mailer encryption. Firstly, the recipient must be using the same e-mailer. Secondly, and even more crucially, you must somehow send the password to the recipient. Sending the password in an ordinary e-mail defeats the purpose of using encryption in the first place.

Public/private key encryption gets around this problem. Encryption is linked to two machine-readable keys: a public key, which can be sent by ordinary e-mail and a private key, which is kept on a local computer. To communicate, both parties exchange public keys by ordinary e-mail. The sender then encrypts a text message using their private key and the public key of the recipient. This encrypted message is then sent to the recipient by e-mail. To decrypt this message the recipient needs their private key and the public key of the sender. This process not only removes the need for sending a password but also means that, using keys, each party can verify that the other party was the sender/recipient.

A freeware program, **Pretty Good Privacy** (PGP), has become the de facto Internet standard for this means of communication. Other uses of public/private key encryption relate to the authentication of messages by appending machine-readable **digital signatures**.

There are two problems. Firstly, you need to trust that an individual's public key really does belong to that person. Secondly, public/private key encryption is viewed askance by some government security agencies as it can defeat their attempts to decrypt messages. This has led to restrictions on its use. It is currently illegal to export PGP from the United States, although PGP is freely available worldwide. There are no current restrictions on its use in the UK. *Cryptography* explains how to obtain and use PGP.

As well as hiding the content of a message, there may also be a need to hide the identity of the sender. Anonymous e-mail is rightly frowned on in some quarters, but it has legitimate uses. For example, it is vital to the Samaritans, who now can be contacted by e-mail and need to preserve the anonymity of their callers.

Anonymous e-mail is achieved using a **remailer**, a computer at an intermediate site which accepts an e-mail with a normal identifier which it strips off before forwarding the e-mail to its intended destination. See the *Anonymous Remailers* FAQ for more information.

Tips on discussion lists
Using the correct address

It is important to distinguish between a mail server address (to which you send subscription requests) and the address of the discussion list itself (to which you send your postings). For example, to subscribe to *PACS-L* (which uses the Listserv mail server), you would send e-mail to:

listserv@uhupvm1.uh.edu

whereas you would send postings to:

pacs-l@uhupvm1.uh.edu

Do not send subscription requests to the discussion list address. When you follow discussion lists, you will see the occasional subscription message incorrectly posted.

If you are responding to a posting on a discussion list, ask yourself whether it is really appropriate to reply to all the participants or just to the original sender. Before you dispatch your reply, check whether your e-mailer is sending it to the discussion list or to the person who posted the message. Some personal replies to postings are inadvertently sent to the entire membership of a discussion list.

Autoreply

If your e-mailer has an **autoreply** feature, to be used, say, to inform people who e-mail you that you are away from work, it is wise not to use it if you subscribe to discussion lists. A message from a mailing list could trigger an autoreply, which goes to the discussion list and is then copied to you as a member of that list, prompting another autoreply, etc. This can create hundreds of 'I am out of the office' messages being sent to every discussion list subscriber very quickly!

List owners

A mail server does not run unattended. A **list owner** is a person who oversees the operation of a particular mail server, usually pertaining to the running of a specific discussion list on that mail server. The list owner will, for example, notify subscribers if postings to a discussion list are lost. A list owner's function is not the same as a moderator of a discussion list, although the two functions can be handled by the same person. The e-mail address of the list owner is usually included in the subscription details for a discussion list.

Discussion list netiquette

Before posting a question to a discussion list, make sure that the answer is not already available as a FAQ. You can ask for responses to your questions to be sent to you personally. Remember to give your e-mail address. Thank any respondents and distribute a brief summary of your answers via the discussion list. The best way to get questions answered is to be known, for example by having replied to other people before. When asking a question, always say how you have tried to find the answer yourself.

If an inflammatory or totally off-topic posting is made to a discussion list you follow, wait at least 24 hours before complaining about it. Other subscribers will probably express the same concerns as you. For a flagrant breach of netiquette (for example an off-topic unsolicited advertisement), you can complain to the list owner of an unmoderated list or, more seriously, to the postmaster at the site where the offending message was posted. If you inadvertently make an off-topic posting to a discussion list, a swift apology should settle things.

Additional features of mail servers

Mail server software can do more than just handle subscription requests. For a complete list of commands that can be given to a particular mail server, send it an e-mail message consisting of the word help.

If an **archive** of previous postings is kept, it may be searchable by commands sent to the mail server. Sometimes associated files for a discussion list (for example a FAQ) can be retrieved via a mail server command. The membership of a discussion list can also be retrieved by e-mail. This is sometimes useful to discover the e-mail address of a particular contributor whom you wish to contact personally.

Dealing with e-mail overload

E-mail can quickly accumulate over holiday periods and at other times when you are unable to read it. While there is nothing you can do about personal messages, e-mail from discussion lists can be temporarily halted. To do this, you need to send a special command to the mail server addresses of each discussion list to which you subscribe, and similarly to resume receiving messages again. Save your subscription confirmation messages for details of how to unsubscribe.

Appropriate commands for different mail servers are also given in James Milles's *Discussion Lists: Mailing List Manager Commands*.

Some discussion lists, if they are particularly busy, offer subscribers a **digest** option which, if chosen, means that you get all the postings made over a time period (typically a day) batched, indexed and sent to you in a single e-mail. While this reduces the number of e-mail messages you receive, digest e-mails can be very large and slow to skim through to get to the postings that interest you.

The main problem with incoming e-mail is that it is usually sorted in order of arrival. This mixes up e-mail from different discussion lists with personal e-mail. A **mail filter** or a **rules-based e-mailer** is software which automatically saves incoming mail to different folders according to rules (instructions) that you define. For example, e-mail from discussion lists can be stored in separate folders, one for each list. This leaves only personal e-mail in your incoming mailbox. If you are short of time, you can just deal with your personal e-mail. The only disadvantage is that you may forget to read and delete e-mail from the other folders. This may cause storage space problems.

A primitive alternative is to acquire more than one e-mail address, for example one for personal e-mail, the other for discussion list e-mail. Ask your Internet access provider if this is permitted. Especially useful for this are the free **web mail** services. A web mail service enables you to pick up and send e-mail from within your web browser. The only disadvantage of this is that you must be online while you read and reply to e-mail. The biggest free web mail provider is MSN's *Hotmail*. The biggest UK-based provider is *Postmaster*.

It is also possible to read certain discussion lists as USENET newsgroups. A good newsreader offering threading is vastly superior to a standard e-mailer. Some discussion lists are widely available in the **bit.listserv.** hierarchy. Check this first for the discussion list you want. Each newsgroup beginning bit.listserv. ends with the name of the discussion list it covers (eg bit.listserv.pacs-l for the *PACS-L* discussion list).

You can ask your Internet service provider to create a newsgroup for the e-mail messages from a discussion list. If a number of people at your site want to read the same discussion list, this economizes on disk space because the messages only need to be stored once at your site (rather than copies in each subscriber's incoming mailbox).

Tips on reading USENET newsgroups

You may not be able to read USENET as your Internet service may not include access to it. In this case there are two options. The first is to access *Deja* via your web browser and use it to read news. The second is to point your newsreader at a public-access news server. *Newzbot* gives a list of these.

Be very selective in choosing which newsgroups to read, and wary about subscribing to newly created newsgroups. You may still find that you cannot read all the newsgroups that you would like. In this case you must order the newsgroups (your newsreader will have a command for this) so that they are displayed to you in priority order. You can then simply work your way down them until you run out of time or inclination. Alternatively you can use *Deja* to look for interesting discussions using keywords.

Deciding which newsgroups to read

Whatever your personal choice of newsgroups, there are a number which are worth considering generally. There are currently only two library/information oriented newsgroups, **soc.libraries.talk** and **comp.internet.library**.

Your Internet access provider or site may provide local newsgroups. If these relate to local user support then they are well worth following.

The **uk.** hierarchy of newsgroups is growing fast. The newsgroup **uk.net.news** is where new newsgroups are discussed and announced.

There are a large number of newsgroups whose names end in **.announce** which cover announcements in a particular area. They are worthwhile because there is no chatter, just a few articles on new Internet resources or information. Your newsreader should allow you to search all newsgroups (not just the ones you subscribe to) for the word 'announce' to find those newsgroups.

Finally, if you find a particularly relevant article in one newsgroup, look to see if it has been **crossposted** (that is posted to a number of newsgroups at once). These other newsgroups might also be of interest to you.

Reading articles and threads

Only read threads that look interesting to you. You do not have to read every article in every thread. Get to recognize who posts articles you find most relevant. Read the initial articles in the longest threads (as these are obviously of interest to the newsgroup audience). Remember to mark all articles as read before you leave the newsgroup, so that next time you will see only new articles.

A facility offered by most newsreaders is the **kill file**. A kill file is a stoplist of subject words or individuals' names which, if attached to an article, prevent that article from appearing in your newsreader. The problem here is to know what to reject.

There are generally two ways of saving interesting articles or threads from your newsreader. The first involves saving them as a file on the computer you use to read USENET. There ought to be a command for **tagging** several articles to save them collectively. The second method sends an article, or a thread, or a set of tagged articles to your e-mail address. You can then deal with the article(s) as e-mail.

Tips on posting to USENET newsgroups

The basic rule is to follow netiquette. Comments made before about posting to discussion lists also apply to posting to newsgroups.

Posting via a newsreader can be tricky. You will need to know the name of the newsgroup (or names, if crossposting). You may need to give a geographical distribution for your message (usually a choice of site, uk or world). You may also be requested to add keywords, but these have little relevance in practice.

There is a newsgroup called **misc.test**, which you can use to practise posting. Use it until you are confident of the posting procedure employed by your newsreader. Your newsreader ought to let you reply to other people's articles. Replies are easier than posting new articles.

Perhaps the easiest way to post to USENET is to use *Deja*. Articles can be submitted directly by registered users or via an e-mail confirmation by unregistered users.

Chapter 6
USING AND CREATING RESOURCES

Tips on using telnet

Once the service is activated you will see a command line interface, and then typically you might enter:

```
telnet site-address
```
(substituting for 'site address' the actual host and domain name or IP address).

Sometimes a **port number** (eg 3000) needs to follow the host/domain name. Once connected, a particular service may require you to **login** using a **public user identifier** and sometimes a password. Often these are shown on the initial 'welcome' screen of the service. The same service may be available at a number of sites; always use the one nearest you, in geographical terms. Try to use a service outside of its normal working hours.

You may be asked to choose a **terminal emulation mode**. This is to allow the remote computer to display text on your computer screen properly. Your telnet client should allow you to choose from a number of terminal emulation modes. The commonest is **VT100**. If in doubt, accept the default offered by the remote system. If the screen looks odd, you have chosen the wrong emulation. Connect to the site again and choose a different terminal emulation.

If you use telnet, then you will need to be familiar with a few basic telnet commands. These can vary because of differences in operating systems and the way that telnet is implemented at different sites. However, the procedures should work on most systems.

Once connected to a remote site (**remote telnet**) then you will need to be familiar with the procedures at that site, or follow the on-screen instructions which are provided by most public-access telnet services. The procedures for disconnecting again vary considerably from site to site. Sometimes instructions are given on the opening screen only, so always make a note of this. This is also true of the **escape sequence** to interrupt the connection in an emergency. Using the escape sequence returns you to **local telnet** (the telnet program on your machine), indicated by the prompt:

```
telnet>
```

You can then use the `quit` or `close` command to disconnect properly.

Tips on using FTP

A user needs a client version of FTP, or you can use a web browser (although dedicated FTP software programs are more reliable if you will be transferring lots of files).

There are a few things to remember, whatever type of client you are using for FTP. The first is to check the size of a file before transferring it. The bigger the file, the longer it will take to transfer. Try transferring a small file first to get an idea of how long bigger files will take. Second, if you find one useful file on an FTP site, there may be more. Look for a file named 'readme', 'index', 'contents' or something similar. This ought to contain a description of all the files in the current directory on the remote site. Sometimes it is worth browsing directory trees on FTP sites, looking for interesting files. To read a text file, you normally transfer it to your own site first, then use a local editor or word processor.

FTP can also be used to transfer files to, rather than from, a remote site. This is known as **uploading**. For security reasons many sites do not allow this. Those sites that do usually have a directory called **incoming** to receive files. Uploaded files should be at least accompanied by a description of their contents and the uploader's name and e-mail address. If considered suitable for the collection at the remote FTP site, uploaded files will be transferred to an appropriate directory. If not, they will almost certainly be deleted.

Anonymous FTP

To start an FTP transfer, you first give the host and domain name of the site to which you want to connect. At the login prompt from the remote site, you enter anonymous. This is the standard response for **anonymous FTP** which allows anyone to log in. Enter your own e-mail address at the password prompt which appears next. This is purely a courtesy, so that the operators of an FTP service know who has used it. Finally, you will see a display of a part of the site's file system, containing files for transfer.

Your FTP client will allow remote files to be chosen and transferred to your site. If you find a 'readme' file, transfer and read this first for further information. Your FTP client will also allow you to move around directories at the remote site, but only those for anonymous FTP. It is good practice to undertake file transfer outside of working hours at the remote site if possible. When you finish you ought to **close**, ie terminate the FTP session properly. You should find the file(s) that you transferred in the directory you were using on your computer before you started your FTP client.

Text and non-text files

Computer files fall into two types: text files and non-text (**binary**) files. Plain text files contain only characters from the **ASCII** character set, which is used by all computers. Thus they can be stored, displayed and printed on any computer, and are reasonably easy to transfer from one computer to another.

Non-text files are always specific to a particular type of computer and possibly operating system as well. To use them in any way almost certainly requires the correct combination of computer and operating system. Transferring non-text files poses more problems than transferring text files.

How do you know whether a file contains just text or not? It is impossible to say from a file name whether the file is a text file or a non-text file. There are **conventions** for filename extensions (the final three characters of the filename) which indicate file format (eg 'txt' for text files), but these conventions can be ignored. If you are using a graphical client, the type of file may be indicated by a suitable icon, but really the only definitive test is to transfer a file and then view it with a **text editor**. If it contains ordinary characters from beginning to end then it is a text file; if it is unreadable or contains unusual characters then it is probably a non-text file. 'Readme' files can be considered to contain text.

You can transfer non-text files using anonymous FTP but you might have to make your client aware that transfers will be of **binary** (non-text) files, rather than **ASCII** (text) files. FTP clients usually default to ASCII transfers. Transferring a file in the wrong mode will render it useless.

File compression

In order to save space on FTP sites, non-text files are usually **compressed** (made smaller by special software which removes repeating elements in a file). Sometimes large text files are compressed, making them into smaller, non-text files. To use any type of compressed file, once you have transferred it to your computer, you need to **decompress** it using special software. Unfortunately there are many ways to compress files for each particular type of computer and thus a whole host of programs is needed to decompress files. The best way to deal with this is to collect as many freeware and shareware decompression programs for your type of computer as you can. Some forms of compression are used a lot more than others (for example 'zipped' files for PCs). See the *comp.compression FAQ* for help.

Finally, if you have downloaded some software, to be on the safe side all such software should be checked for viruses before running it. Excellent **virus checkers** are also available from software archives. See the *McAffee.com Anti Virus Center* for help on viruses.

Tips on using the web
Working with URLs

If you have a web browser you can 'open' a link to any page on the Internet, providing you know its URL. Use the 'open' command or its equivalent and enter the URL. If you get 'Not found' or a similar error message, first check that you have entered the URL *exactly* as it should be, character for character and case for case. There are no spaces in URLs. Don't worry about typing http:// as your browser should automatically add it on to the address. If you have not made a mistake, try truncating the URL by omitting characters from the right-hand end, up to the rightmost slash (/). For example, instead of

http://www.vnu.co.uk/vnu/pcw/bob.htm

try using

http://www.vnu.co.uk/vnu/pcw/

If your truncated URL still does not work, keep removing the last portion until you reach the slash that precedes the site name. If this still fails there is no point in truncating further. All truncation is doing is looking for higher-level pages at the site in question. If you find a URL that works, you may be able to follow links to the page you want. However, do be prepared for invalid URLs, for URLs which point to non-existent pages, or for sites which are not available when you want to use them. It is sometimes possible to guess URLs if you are familiar with the main domain types – eg the URL for IBM computers is **http://www.ibm.com/** (not all URLs are so obvious though).

You will find that many URLs end in a slash symbol. This means that the page they refer to has a **default** (expected) name, like home.html or index.htm. The names of pages must comply with the file-naming conventions of the computer where they are kept. Thus **home.html** cannot be stored on a computer running Windows, as file extensions (.html in this case) can only be up to three letters long on this operating system.

Retrieving non-text files

Some links lead to individual graphics (graphics on pages are called **inline graph-ics**), or pieces of sound or video. Your browser needs extra software to handle these formats. Most browsers have a customizable list of file extensions which call up an appropriate piece of software (known as a **viewer** or **helper** or **plug-in**) when a file with a certain extension is retrieved. Plug-ins need to be downloaded and installed: a large collection is available from the *BrowserWatch Plug-In Plaza*. Whether sound can be heard or not is also dependent on your computer.

Storing URLs

If you find an interesting page or website you can return easily to the same loca-tion on another occasion by storing it in your browser's hotlist – this is known as **bookmarks** in *Netscape* or **favorites** in Internet Explorer. Think of this as your own personal address book for the web. You can also share bookmarks or favourites with other users or computers.

Saving information

You can store pages on the computer which is running your browser by setting the browser to load pages to disk or using a 'save as' option if your browser has one. Pages which you have loaded to disk can be reloaded later without having to be connected to the Internet. Some browsers allow you to e-mail a page to your-self. It is possible to save images alone to disk by right-clicking on the image and following the pop-menu which should appear.

You may just want to **print** out a page of information: this will print with all the formatting that you see on screen but without the colour (unless you are using a colour printer).

If you just want to take a quote or a few lines of text from a web page you can **copy** and **paste** text from the screen by simply highlighting the text and using the edit menu to copy – this can then be pasted into any text document.

Improving response times

Pages can sometimes take many minutes to load. Speed of page retrieval depends partly on where the page is coming from. Retrieving a page from the USA is often slow compared to a European site and takes longer later in the day. Use a nearby mirror site if you can find one, and choose a time of day that is likely to be quiet at the remote site.

There are two other ways of speeding up page retrieval. The first is to stop your browser loading graphics. Graphics are nice, but take far longer to load than the textual content of pages. The second way to speed things up is to use a **caching proxy**. This is a special computer which stores a copy of the page(s) that you retrieve. If you go back to those pages, or reload them, your browser will load them from the caching proxy computer, and not the original source. You will need to ask your Internet access provider about the availability of a caching proxy (most academic institutions should run one).

Using a web browser for other tasks

As well as http (**hypertext transfer protocol**), your browser can also perform tasks like telnet connection, FTP, Gopher browsing and reading files stored on your computer. This is done by replacing the **http://** task at the beginning of a URL with another task name:

telnet://   opens a telnet connection to a site whose name follows. Your browser will need external telnet software to run the telnet session. This can be called up in the same way as viewers/helpers.

ftp://   opens an anonymous FTP session to a site whose name follows. The site name may be followed by a directory path and a filename, to retrieve a specific file. If no filename is given it is possible to browse the directory tree on the remote FTP server and select files for transfer.

gopher://   opens a Gopher session to a Gopher whose site name follows. The site name may be followed by a path to a particular page which often bears some relation to the menu headings that lead to the same page from the top level menu at the site.

file://   followed by a directory path and a filename retrieves a file from the computer which is running your browser.

Privacy and the web

Your browser can allow the sites you browse to collect information about you (your home site, e-mail address, name, the computer you are using etc.). If this bothers you then use the *Anonymous Surfing* resource.

Searching the Internet

The basic software required to search the Internet is an e-mailer and a web browser. A newsreader is an optional extra. Experience and confidence with these are essential. The latest web browsers include e-mail and newsreader facilities built into the software.

The Internet should be seen as an addition to the existing range of traditional information sources, yet its very nature makes it unreliable for quick reference work in a library. Even if you know of a site that could contain information to answer a patron's request, and you have the necessary client software to access it, there is no guarantee that the site will be operational, or that your Internet connection will be functioning at the time you need it. Even if things are working, the speed of response might be too slow because of network overload. If you know of an individual, or more likely a discussion list, where an answer to a patron's request might be obtained by e-mail, it is very unlikely that a response will be forthcoming immediately.

So why bother with searching the Internet? It offers a staggering range of data, information and software, covering almost every subject imaginable. The vast majority of this information is free. Because it is free it can be unfavourably compared, for example, with conventional reference books for authority, coverage and consistency, but in a sense this is not comparing like with like. The power of the Internet as an information resource lies in information that is not available or not available from the same perspective elsewhere, and, importantly, information that is not easily accessible to the public at large by other means. Its major strength lies in the huge diversity of material available, aimed at all subjects, all levels and all types of user. A vast amount of information has been compiled by enthusiasts, volunteers and interested parties; as an information resource reflecting the spectrum of modern culture, society and human endeavour, the Internet is thus unparalleled. Volunteer information providers (mainly individuals) often include a disclaimer about the accuracy and comprehensiveness of their data, yet the quality *can* be admirable.

Much information is supplied in good faith and may have a copyright notice which sets clear limits on how the data can be used. But usage is almost impossible to police, as users can make their own copy of any information resource. Mainstream publishers are wary of using the Internet for anything more than sales and advertising, through fears of piracy.

The first thing to decide is whether a traditional source will give you the information you require. The Internet can function as a gateway to library OPACs and to collections of library-based resources (like *CARL*). However, the Internet comes into its own when traditional sources fail.

The basic resources are covered under Subject listings and search engines (p88) in the Resource Guide. The best way to start is to investigate a general subject listing, like *Yahoo!* or *BUBL LINK* (which is maintained in DDC order by librarian volunteers) or collections of subject resources, like those maintained by the **subject gateways** in the UK *Resource Discovery Network*.

If browsing directories fails to turn up anything, then try a searchable index, like *Lycos*, *AltaVista*, *Infoseek* or *Hotbot*. Since these are machine-generated indexes they can include more resources than can the subject listings. With no keyword control, however, you are searching a vast amount of free-text; misses and false drops due to the vagaries of word usage are almost inevitable. You need to strike a balance between combining too many search terms and too few. Each searchable index (or **search engine**) differs in the searching facilities it offers. Be sure to read any available help file.

Some searchable indexes specialize in indexing particular types of information: eg *Whoopie* provides an index of video and audio files and *WhoWhere?* provides access to e-mail, phone and postal addresses. Services like *All-in-one* collect and group searchable indexes by category. Whilst it is not possible to go into great detail here about the different merits of all these services, Richard Eskin's *Search Tools: a Guide* at Manchester Metropolitan University's site will provide you with a comprehensive introduction to search tools available and pointers to tutorials on using search engines effectively.

Even the machine-generated indexes cannot cover everything. The last resort is asking by e-mail or USENET for either pointers to resources, or just for the information you require. This is the step that takes the most amount of time, as you have to identify relevant discussion lists or USENET newsgroups first, and then follow them to make sure that they cover your topic properly and that your question is not a common one. However, if you locate the correct forum, you can be sure to get some sort of an answer to your question. No response probably means that no one knows. When all else fails, the *STUMPERS-L* discussion list is for questions that no one else can answer; it is of course populated by reference librarians!

If searching is arduous for the librarian, then what about end-user searching? The appeal of the Internet for the end-user is that not finding what they want is very often offset by finding something of equal interest that they did not know they wanted. The Internet is also seductively available for the end-user, as it comes to their office or home computer. This is not yet a threat to the library; the Internet contains very different types of information and does not offer access to that information in a straightforward and dependable manner.

Some general search tips

Different search engines and services use different rules for searching – for best results read the help files they provide and get to know the capabilities of one or two search engines really well. However, some very general rules for searching are:

- Take some time to think about what you are actually searching for before you begin and try to formulate a search strategy.
- Try to be specific with the keywords that you use: if you are interested in pho-

tography specify what area, eg composition, equipment, etc. There are millions of web pages out there, so generally the more specific you can be the better.

- If your search returned few or no results think about possible synonyms.
- Use the options of combining words with 'and': ie searching on photography **and** equipment will look for documents containing **both** those terms.
- Some search engines will let you search using 'not' – a search for photography **not** equipment will look for documents containing the word photography but not containing the word equipment.
- If you are searching for proper names use capitalization, which should narrow down the results. If you type in lower case most search engines will search both upper and lower case words.
- Review your initial search results and refine your search terms if necessary.

How to keep up to date with resources on the Internet

Keeping up to date is essentially a matter of following appropriate discussion lists and USENET newsgroups. You will find that other people announce their own new resources, or recommend ones which they themselves have used. The problem is how to store these recommendations so that you can act on them later, as the need arises or the time becomes available?

If you can locate a couple of information servers that cover your interests, you are in luck. All you need to do is **bookmark** these sites in your web browser and return to them occasionally to check whether they have been updated since your last visit; alternatively you can use a notification service such as *Mind-it* which will notify you when web pages have changed. Making your bookmark file your **home page** will give you quick access to those sites you find most useful every time you open up your browser.

Web agents are services that ask you to type in keywords about your areas of interest, and then send you regular e-mails with URLs that contain those words. These rely on automated searches and so do not always yield quality sites. *The Informant* lets you save search engine queries and favourite websites, which it periodically checks, and notifies you of updates. Alternatively **personal search engines** run from your own machine and can be configured to search a range of search engines using one or more search statements. They will then try to automatically sort and organize the results. It is recommended you use them for overnight searches! *TUCOWS* is a good source of personal search engines, like Web-Compass and Web-Ferret.

What if you cannot find existing information servers which cover your topics and which are kept up to date? You are then left with raw announcements from discussion lists and newsgroups. Printing these out for future reference is hopeless unless you have all the time in the world to spend filing ephemera.

Organizing messages into appropriately named folders on your computer is marginally better, but it is worth being ruthless about deleting anything you have not acted on after a period of time. In all likelihood, the information will have been superseded.

In fact, all you really need to store are e-mail addresses and web URLs, as the latter can accommodate all the existing range of Internet file resources. The best solution is to learn to build a web page in HTML and to use it as a personal repository of up-to-date resources. You do not need a home page on a web server to do this. Your web browser can retrieve a page stored as a local file on the computer you use to access the Internet. Thus, when online, all your references are immediately available and, if they are URLs, immediately useable as well.

If you think your resource page is worthy enough, then publish it by putting it on a web server as a home page. Ask your Internet access provider about access to web server space. If you announce your web home page through discussion lists and newsgroups, you will find that people will comment on your page, and maybe point out resources that you have missed. They may also let you know by personal e-mail about resources they find. The best way to stay up to date is to become a well-known and well-respected information provider yourself!

Building a web page

Building a web page is a straightforward task. HTML (hypertext markup language) is a set of **tags**, ie matched pairs of markers, which delineate particular features on a page. The basic structure of an HTML page is:

```
<HTML>
<HEADER>
<TITLE>Example HTML page</TITLE>
</HEADER>
<BODY>
This is an example HTML page.
</BODY>
</HTML>
```

Tags are never seen when the page is viewed by a browser. In the above example 'Example HTML page' would appear in the browser window title and 'This is an example HTML page' in the browser window itself. Each tag names the feature it delineates. The effect of a pair of tags is limited to the material between them. Some tags, however, are unitary; for example <P> marks the end of a paragraph. Tags are clearly explained in *HyperText Markup Language (HTML): Working and Background Materials*.

Markup tags can be added to text by using a text editor or a word processor. Add-ons have been released for leading word processors, to enable them to save material in HTML format. Software is available which converts files from formats like **RTF** (rich text format) to HTML, as are dedicated HTML editors. If you intend to add graphics to your pages then you will need graphic editing and conversion software. Guides to HTML and associated software are referenced from the *W3C* site.

A good way of picking up expertise is to use your browser to view the **source** (i.e the HTML markup) of any pages which strike you as being well designed or eye-catching. Remember that your browser can also save retrieved pages in HTML format to the computer on which your browser is running. These can then be examined to see how they work.

It is a good idea to test out your own pages by using your browser to look at your pages as local files (using the file:// task name at the start of the URL). Browsers, though, may require the presence of an Internet link to work, so that making a browser work in **local mode** can be tricky.

Making links between your own pages can be a chore if you enter the full URL for each link. **Relative URLs** (usually just a pathname and/or filename) cause your browser to use the root of the last full URL referenced. Thus, if your first page is referenced as

file://C:/html/home.htm

then another page, stored in the file **next.htm** in the same directory, only needs to be referenced by the relative URL **next.htm**. The browser automatically assumes that the full URL is

file://C:/html/next.htm

You will find that relative links also make your pages easier to move around as a collection between different hosts, without having to change all the URLs that link to them.

If you intend to put your pages on a web server for other people to access, try to view your pages first using as many different browsers as you can. You will find that browsers all have idiosyncrasies in the way they render HTML files on screen. Some browsers have various extra tags that they can render; be wary of using these as different browsers cannot interpret them. Finally, consider how your pages look without inline graphics.

PART 4
Internet Resource Guide

Contents

IV

Introduction 70

Resources linked to Part 1 73

Resources linked to Part 2 79

Resources from other organizations 117

Resources linked to Part 3 131

Introduction to Part 4

How to read the Resource Guide

The Resource Guide is organized into broad sections by topics which generally follow their sequence in the main text. Within each section, resources are arranged alphabetically by name and incorporate everything cited in the main text along with additional resources relevant to the section. To locate useful resources, browse the entries in the appropriate section(s).

If the resource sought has a recognized name, then it will be locatable via the index to the book.

Each resource is described according to a standard template, an annotated version of which is shown on the following page to explain the entries in the main guide and how to use them.

Throughout, italics have been used to indicate where you should substitute your own information, such as your name or e-mail address.

For most resources, including information servers and FTP sites, access details are expressed in terms of URLs. If a resource is also (or only) available via telnet, then a site-address and public user identifier (to login via telnet) are also given. Resources were last checked in October 1999. Details may have changed since then.

Annotated template, explaining entries in the Resource Guide

Name		**Common abbreviation (if any) and full name of the resource**
ISSN		(for e-journals only)
Provider		Organizational and/or personal name of the provider (countries have only been given where appropriate).
Description		Factual description of the resource.
Comments		Impressionistic comments about content, organization or access to the resource.
Access	URL	One or more URLs, giving a UK or European location if available. Some resources are available by several methods (**http://**, **ftp://**, etc), in which case URLs for each are shown
	Telnet	Site address(es) with host and domain name(s); IP address may also be given. (Use with command line telnet client, eg `telnet site-address` or construct a URL as follows: `telnet://site-address/`)
	Login	The public user identifier for the remote system (type this at the login: prompt)
	Path	Menu path to the resource for basic telnet users
	Logout	Disconnect command for basic telnet users
	E-mail	E-mail address (if given, send a message to this e-mail address to receive a plain-text copy of the resource by e-mail. Leave the subject line blank)
	Message	Text of the message that you should send
Subscription details		
	E-mail	E-mail address of mail server for discussion lists and e-journals (send a message to this e-mail address to subscribe; leave the subject line blank)
	Message	Text of the message that you should send to subscribe (substitute your own details for anything in italics, eg Jane Smith for *your-firstname your-lastname*)

RESOURCES LINKED TO PART 1

Networking organizations

Name **Electronic Commerce and the European Union**
Provider European Union
Description Comprehensive and up-to-date collection of information on various commercial and governmental e-commerce initiatives in Europe.
Access URL **http://www.ispo.cec.be/ecommerce/Welcome.html**

Name **Electronic Frontier Foundation**
Provider EFF: Electronic Frontier Foundation (USA)
Description The Electronic Frontier Foundation is a civil liberties pressure group for Internet-related issues, such as individual privacy and freedom of expression. Its file archives contain a wealth of material on its activities and related areas. It publishes a newsletter, *EFFector online*, distributed on the USENET group comp.org.eff.news. The EFF's (extended) guide to the Internet is freely available at this site. EFF activities and related issues are debated on the USENET group **comp.org.eff.talk**.
Comments A pioneering organization; membership is open to interested parties.
Access URLs **http://www.eff.org/**
      ftp://ftp.eff.org/
      news:comp.org.eff.news
      news:comp.org.eff.talk

Name **The Electronic Libraries Programme**
Provider UKOLN: the UK Office for Library and Information Networking
Description The UK-based Electronic Libraries Programme (eLib) is a major research effort investigating the electronic/digital library. Background to the Programme, and links to all current and past projects, are on the web server.
Access URL **http://www.ukoln.ac.uk/services/elib/**

Name **ICANN Home Page**
Provider ICANN (Internet Corporation for Assigned Names and Numbers)
Description Independent organization that now controls the DNS (Domain Name System).
Access URL **http://www.icann.org/**

Name	**IETF: Internet Engineering Task Force**
Provider	IETF Secretariat
Description	'The Internet Engineering Task Force is a loosely self-organized group of people who make technical and other contributions to the engineering and evolution of the Internet and its technologies.' The IETF provides Internet management, standards and technical information, and many sources of further information.
Access	URLs **http://www.ietf.cnri.reston.va.us/** **ftp://ietf.cnri.reston.va.us/**

Name	**InetUK: UK Internet Access Providers**
Provider	ArcGlade Services Ltd
Description	Names, addresses, contact details plus a summary of the services, fees and resources of UK Internet access providers.
Access	URL **http://www.limitless.co.uk/inetuk/providers.html**

Name	**Internet Cafe Guide**
Provider	Ernst Larsen
Description	Guide to Internet cybercafes worldwide. Strong on the UK.
Access	URL **http://www.netcafeguide.com/**

Name	**Internet Domain Survey**
Provider	Internet Software Consortium
Description	Conducts regular searches to try to discover every host on the Internet.
Access	URL **http://www.isc.org/ds/**

Name	**Internet Society Home Page**
Provider	Internet Society
Description	Contains information, activities and corporate membership of the Internet Society as well as much information about the Internet (administration, funding, codes of conduct, key organizations, usage statistics).
Access	URLs **http://info.isoc.org/** **ftp://ftp.isoc.org/**

Name   **Internet Watch Foundation**

Provider   Internet Watch Foundation/Peter Dawe

Description   Independent organization dedicated to the removal of illegal material from the Internet. Runs a hotline for reporting such material.

Access   URL   **http://www.internetwatch.org.uk/**

Name   **JANET Information Server**

Provider   UKERNA: United Kingdom Educational and Research Networking Association

Description   Contains a wealth of information and documentation on JANET and SuperJANET, including policy and technical documents, JANET sites and servers, major UK national networking facilities and the registration of **ac.uk** domain names. Incorporates the newsletter *JANET.news*.

Access   URL   **http://www.ja.net/**

             E-mail   **infoserv@news.janet.ac.uk**

             Message   **request index** (for an index of documents)

                         request reference-number (for a specific document number from the index)

Name   **JISC**

Provider   Joint Information Systems Committee (UK)

Description   Conducts research into various networking applications in higher education. Contains information and documentation on the JISC, including policy and technical documents, JISC-funded sites and servers, and a useful glossary of networking terms and organizations.

Access   URL   **http://www.jisc.ac.uk/**

Name   **Network Solutions**

Provider   Network Solutions, Inc

Description   Under the auspices of *ICANN*, this company operates the DNS (Domain Name System).

Access   URL   **http://www.networksolutions.com/**

Name   **Nominet UK Network Information Centre**

Provider   Nominet UK

Description   Company that controls the assignment of names in the **.uk** domain.

Access   URL   **http://www.nominet.org.uk/**

Name　　**NUA Internet Surveys**
Provider　NUA
Description　Comprehensive collection of data relating to all aspects of the Internet.
Access　　URL　**http://www.nua.ie/surveys/**

Name　　**TERENA: Trans-European Research and Education Networking Association**
Provider　TERENA Secretariat
Description　Information about TERENA and its predecessor, EARN (European Academic and Research Network). Also, Europe-wide networking initiatives, including reports, calls for proposals, conference papers and abstracts. Also contains documentation for major Internet tools, much of which comes from the former EARN, and links to international networking centres (eg InterNic).
Access　　URL　**http://www.terena.nl/**

Name　　**uk.telecom FAQ**
Provider　James Grinter
Description　Exhaustive guide to all things telecom-related in the UK. It is worth following the uk-telecom newsgroup to keep up with advances.
Access　　URLs　**http://www.gbnet.net/net/uk-telecom/**
　　　　　　http://www.lib.ox.ac.uk/internet/news/faq/uk.
　　　　　　　telecom.html
　　　　　　http://www.faqs.org/faqs/by-newsgroup/uk/
　　　　　　　uk.telecom.html

Name　　**W3C: the World Wide Web Consortium**
Provider　The Laboratory for Computer Science at MIT (Massachusetts Institute of Technology, INRIA (Institut National de Recherche en Informatique et en Automatique) and Keio University, with support from DARPA (Defense Advanced Research Projects Agency) and the European Commission
Description　The W3C was founded in 1994 to develop common standards for the evolution of the world wide web. It is the source for any technical or background information relating to the web itself. The director of the W3C is Tim Berners-Lee, the creator of the world wide web.
Access　　URL　**http://www.w3.org/**

RESOURCES LINKED TO PART 2

Discussion lists and electronic conferences

Name   **Computer Telephony Portal**
Provider   Ken Persson
Description Exhaustive guide to communicating by telephone over the Internet. Includes links to mailing lists, newsgroups and conferences on the topic.
Access   URL   **http://www.computertelephony.org/**

Name   **Deja: the Source for Internet Newsgroups**
Provider   Deja Inc
Description Has the largest collection of archived USENET newsgroups, with coverage going back to March 1995. Allows posting.
Access   URL   **http://www.deja.com/**

Name   **Delphi Forums**
Provider   Delphi Forums, Inc
Description Used to be an online service, much like America Online. Has relaunched as a conferencing system, offering free access and the ability to create new conferences.
Access   URL   **http://www.delphi.com/**

Name   **Directory of Scholarly and Professional E-Conferences**
Provider   Diane K. Kovacs and team, Kent State University Libraries (USA)
Description Provides descriptions and subscription information of more than 2000 academic discussion lists and newsgroups, listed by subject category. Descriptions can also be searched by keyword.
Comments   Includes a large number of established lists in the library and information sector, including UK lists on Mailbase. An annual print version is published by the Association of Research Libraries.
Access   URL   **http://n2h2.com/KOVACS/**

Name   **Discussion Lists: Mailing List Manager Commands**
Provider   James Milles, Saint Louis University Law Library (USA)
Description Summary of commands for five widely used mail server programs used to manage Internet discussion lists: Listserv, Listproc, Mailbase, Mailserv and Majordomo.
Access   URL   **http://lawwww.cwru.edu/cwrulaw/faculty/milles/ mailser.html**

Name   **Fight Spam on the Internet!**

Provider   CAUCE (Campaign Against Unsolicited Commercial Email)

Description   Great campaigning site that offers a number of ways to fight Spam.

Access   URL   **http://spam.abuse.net/**

Name   **Forum One**

Provider   Forum One Communications Corporation

Description   Provides a name search capability for, and directory access to, over 300,000 web forums and conferencing sites.

Access   URL   **http://www.forumone.com/**

Name   **ICQ**

Provider   ICQ, Inc

Description   Provides copious information on how to use ICQ, links to various meeting places, 'topic rings', and of course the package itself and various add-ons.

Access   URL   **http://www.icq.com/**

Name   **Internet FAQ Consortium**

Provider   Kent Landfield

Description   Provides access to a complete listing of USENET FAQs.

Access   URL   **http://www.faqs.org/**

Name   **Internet Relay Chat Help Site**

Provider   Irchelp.org

Description   Everything you need to use chat, including a tutorial, a primer, FAQs, information on channels, links to IRC clients and more.

Access   URL   **http://www.irchelp.org/**

Name   **JESSE**

Provider   Gretchen Whitney, University of Tennessee (USA)

Description   An open forum for discussion of library and information science education.

Comments   Almost all postings are from the USA.

Subscription details

    E-mail   **listserv@utkvm1.utk.edu**

    Message   **subscribe jesse** *your-firstname your-lastname*

Name	**Library-Oriented Lists and Electronic Serials**
Provider	Washington Research Library Consortium (WRLC)
Description	A full-text document listing a considerable number of BITNET (Because It's Time Network) and Internet lists and e-journals in the library and information sector, giving target audience for each and brief instructions for subscribing.
Comments	Includes Listserv, Listproc and other types of list, but not Mailbase. Can be retrieved by e-mailing the listserv address given below. The web server provides a useful subject index and indicates which lists can be read as USENET newsgroups.
Access	URL **http://www.wrlc.org/liblists/**

Name	**LIS-BAILER**	
Provider	BAILER: British Association for Information and Library Education and Research	
Description	Aimed at lecturers and research staff in departments of library and information studies.	
Access	URL	**http://www.mailbase.ac.uk/lists/lis-bailer/**
Subscription details		
	E-mail	**mailbase@mailbase.ac.uk**
	Message	**join lis-bailer** *your-firstname your-lastname*

Name	**LIS-FID**	
Provider	Staff of Queen Margaret College, Edinburgh, on behalf of the International Federation for Information and Documentation (Netherlands)	
Description	Aims to promote discussion of information management and library and information science in an international context.	
Access	URL	**http://www.mailbase.ac.uk/lists/lis-fid/**
Subscription details		
	E-mail	**mailbase@mailbase.ac.uk**
	Message	**join lis-fid** *your-firstname your-lastname*

Name	**LIS-IIS**	
Provider	Members of the Institute of Information Scientists (UK)	
Description	This list is open to anyone interested in discussing information science issues.	
Access	URL	**http://www.mailbase.ac.uk/lists/lis-iis/**
Subscription details		
	E-mail	**mailbase@mailbase.ac.uk**
	Message	**join lis-iis** *your-firstname your-lastname*

Name   **LIS-link**

Provider   Mailbase (UK)

Description   Generally recognized as the key list for news, announcements and discussion of general interest to the UK library and information community. Postings cover wide-ranging topics within the general sphere of library and information work. Used by BUBL to distribute regular update bulletins.

Access   URL   **http://www.mailbase.ac.uk/lists/lis-link/**

Subscription details

    E-mail   **mailbase@mailbase.ac.uk**

    Message   **join LIS-link** *your-firstname your-lastname*

Name   **LISSPS: Library and Information Studies Students and Prospective Students**

Provider   Andrew Brown and UKOLN

Description   An information server and discussion list aimed at students on, and potential applicants to, LIS courses.

Access   URL   **http://hosted.ukoln.ac.uk/lissps/**

Subscription details

    E-mail   **majordomo@ukoln.bath.ac.uk**

    Message   **subscribe lissps**

Name   **Liszt: the Mailing List Directory**

Provider   Scott Southwick

Description   Searchable directory of over 90,000 mailing lists, updated weekly.

Access   URL   **http://www.liszt.com/**

    E-mail   **liszter@bluemarble.net**

    Message   **help** (for listing of search commands)

Name **Mailbase Mailing List Service**
Provider   Mailbase (UK)
Description   Provides a complete alphabetical listing of all Mailbase discussion lists, with further information including joining instructions, owners and moderators, members and mail archives for each list. Also Mailbase documentation including instructions for setting up a list.
Comments   As list names are seldom meaningful, the alphabetical index is only useful to locate information about a known list. However, there is an index of list names and descriptions to search for lists on a topic. It is also possible to search the membership of all Mailbase lists to locate a person's e-mail address, and to search the archives of a specified list.
Access   URL   **http://www.mailbase.ac.uk/**

Name **Network News**
Provider   University of Oxford
Description   A major UK repository of USENET newsgroup FAQs, listed by name and by category. The archive can also be searched by keyword.
Access   URL   **http://www.lib.ox.ac.uk/internet/news/**

Name **New-List**
Provider   Gleason Sackman, Internet Scout Project (USA)
Description   Informs subscribers of new Listserv lists as they are created.
Subscription details
      E-mail   **listserv@hypatia.cs.wisc.edu**
      Message   **subscribe new-list** *your-firstname your-lastname*

Name **New-Lists**
Provider   Mailbase (UK)
Description   Informs subscribers of new Mailbase lists as they are created.
Access   URL   **http://www.mailbase.ac.uk/lists/new-lists/**
Subscription details
      E-mail   **mailbase@mailbase.ac.uk**
      Message   **join new-lists** *your-firstname your-lastname*

Name **Onnow**
Provider   Talk City, Inc
Description   A comprehensive guide to events on the Internet happening today, tomorrow and beyond, across a wide variety of topics, from Music to Sports to Technology.
Access   URL   **http://www.onnow.com/**

Name	**ORBS (Open Relay Blocking System)**
Provider	Alan Brown
Description	ORBS maintains a blacklist of sites with open e-mail relays, which can be used to send spam e-mail. If you get e-mails returned with a warning they are using a site blacklisted by ORBS, you must contact your Internet access provider immediately, as only they can remove the blacklisting.
Access	URL **http://www.orbs.org/**

Name	**PACS-L: the Public Access Computer Systems Forum**
Providers	Nancy Buchanan, Linda Thompson, Jack Hall, University of Houston (USA)
Description	One of the largest library-oriented lists, PACS-L handles discussion on end-user computer systems of all types of libraries. Subscribers also receive *Current Cites*, *PACS-News*, *PACS-Review* and the *LITA Newsletter* (electronic journals).
Access	URL **http://www.lib.uh.edu/pacsl.html**
Subscription details	
	E-mail **listserv@uhupvm1.uh.edu**
	Message **subscribe pacs-l** *your-firstname your-lastname*

Name	**PAML: Publicly Accessible Mailing Lists**
Provider	Stephanie da Silva
Description	A massive, multidisciplinary collection of discussion lists, arranged by name and by subject keywords on the web server.
Access	URLs **http://www.neosoft.com/internet/paml/**
	ftp://rtfm.mit.edu/pub/usenet/news.answers/mail/ mailing-lists/part01 [-22]
	E-mail **listserv@listserv.taronga.com**
	Message **subscribe paml-updates** *your-firstname your-lastname*

Name	**STUMPERS-L**
Provider	Concordia University (USA)
Description	Challenging reference questions (a list for librarians only).
Access	URL **http://www.cuis.edu/~stumpers/**
Subscription details	
	E-mail **mailserv@crf.cuis.edu**
	Message **subscribe stumpers-l** *your-e-mail address*

Name   **TILE.NET**

Provider   Lyris Technologies, Inc

Description   Complete index to USENET newsgroups, Listserv discussion lists, FTP sites and computer product vendors, listed by name and by category. Gives a short description of each group, brief usage statistics and access details (where known).

Access   URL   **http://tile.net/**

Name   **Video Conferencing Cookbook**

Provider   Southeastern Universities Research Association Video Development Initiative (USA)

Description   Step-by-step guide to using videoconferencing in higher education.

Access   URL   **http://sunsite.utk.edu/video_cookbook/**

Name   **Web4Lib**

Provider   Information Systems Instruction and Support, University of California at Berkeley Library (USA)

Description   Aimed at librarians who are involved in the creation and management of library-based web servers and clients.

Access   URL   **http://sunsite.berkeley.edu/Web4Lib/**

Subscription details

                E-mail   **listserv@library.berkeley.edu**

                Message   **subscribe web4lib** *your-firstname your-lastname*

Subject listings and search engines

Name   **Ahoy: The Homepage Gateway**

Provider   Jonathan Shakes, Marc Langheinrich and Professor Oren Etzioni at the University of Washington (USA)

Description Uses Metacrawler to create a list of possible pages and then 'sifts' the results, looking for the most likely matches for the person sought. Also finds e-mail addresses.

Access   URL   **http://ahoy.cs.washington.edu:6060/**

Name   **All-in-One Search Page**

Provider   William Cross

Description An exhaustive listing of forms-based search tools assembled on one page for easy access. Search tools are categorized under headings (WWW, people, software, news/weather, publications, documentation etc).

Access   URL   **http://www.allonesearch.com/**

Name   **AltaVista**

Provider   AltaVista

Description Gives access to a searchable database of over 140 million web pages and 4 million USENET postings. Boolean operators are supported, searches can be limited to parts of web pages, images, videos, audio files or USENET postings, and advanced options allow features like preferential weighting of certain search words.

Access   URL   **http://www.altavista.com/**

Name   **ArchiePlex**

Provider   Created by NEXOR and maintained by EMNET (UK)

Description An Archie gateway for the world wide web to help locate files on ftp sites around the world.

Access   URLs   **http://archie.emnet.co.uk/**
                     http://www.funet.fi/funet/archie/archieplexform.html
                     http://www.lerc.nasa.gov/archieplex/

Name   **ARGUS Clearinghouse**
Provider   Argus Associates, Inc.
Description Acts as a repository for subject resource guides compiled by members of the Internet community and by students of the School of Information and Library Studies at the University of Michigan.
Comments   Offers hierarchical subject browsing and keyword searching.
Access   URL   **http://www.clearinghouse.net/**

Name   **ASK Jeeves**
Provider   Ask Jeeves, Inc.
Description Attempts to provide natural language searching of web sites and documents by storing searches from previous users and building up a databank of answers.
Access   URL   **http://www.askjeeves.com/**

Name   **Big Foot UK**
Provider   Big Foot
Description Searchable directory of e-mail names and addresses.
Access   URL   **http://www.bigfoot.co.uk/**

Name   **BUBL LINK**
Provider   BUBL Information Service (UK)
Description A listing of selected Internet resources. The resource lists are compiled by a growing number of volunteers at different sites, with the intention of providing a service to academics and researchers as well as to librarians.
Comments   Subject tree is arranged by DDC number, and subject headings can be searched by keyword. Alternatively, subjects are listed alphabetically.
Access   URL   **http://bubl.ac.uk/link/**

Name   **BUBL Search**
Provider   BUBL Information Service (UK)
Description Provides for searching of BUBL files. Offers a good selection of searchable indexes for Internet resources generally and by category.
Access   URL   **http://bubl.ac.uk/searches/**

Name   **Dogpile**
Provider   Dogpile, Inc
Description Useful meta search engine with an unforgettable name!
Access   URL   **http://www.dogpile.com/**

Name   **Excite**
Provider   Excite, Inc
Description Searchable database of millions of web pages. Also provides person-
             alization features to provide your own interface to information,
             including news, weather, sports and horoscope information
Access   URL   **http://www.excite.com/**

Name   **Google**
Provider   Google, Inc
Description Searchable database with a difference: uses a mathematical formula
             to look at the number of citations a web page has in relation to other
             pages and ranks results based on the calculation. Also caches the web
             pages for faster access. This novel approach can produce useful
             results.
Access   URL   **http://www.google.com/**

Name   **HotBot**
Provider   Hotwired
Description Gives access to a searchable database of some 110 million web pages.
             Searches can contain Boolean operators and may be limited to parts
             of web pages. Searching of USENET postings is also offered.
Access   URL   **http://www.hotbot.com/**

Name   **The Informant**
Provider   Push Technologies
Description A free service that will save your search engine queries and web sites,
             check them periodically, and send you e-mail whenever there are
             new or updated web pages.
Access   URL   **http://informant.dartmouth.edu/**

Name   **Infoseek**
Provider   Infoseek Corp.
Description Combines a searchable database of web pages with a directory
             approach to resources by subject. Searching options go from basic to
             advanced, with related concepts being suggested.
Access   URL   **http://infoseek.go.com/**

Name   **Lycos: Your Personal Internet Guide**

Provider   Lycos, Inc

Description Indexes the texts of several million web pages. Sounds and images from those pages are also searchable. Words and prefixes can be used as search terms. Boolean AND and NOT searching is offered

Access   URL   **http://www-uk.lycos.com/**

Name   **Metacrawler**

Provider   Go2Net, Inc

Description Meta search engine that sends a user's query to over ten of the top search engines, results are formatted and ranked according to relevance.

Access   URL   **http://www.go2net.com/search.html**

Name   **NISS Directory of Networked Resources**

Provider   NISS (UK)

Description Provides descriptions of and access to information sources worldwide. Resources are arranged by UDC number, normally to the two-digit level.

Comments In contrast to many subject listings, provides descriptions, written by subject experts, of resources. These descriptions are searchable by keyword.

Access   URL   **http://www.niss.ac.uk/subject/**

Name   **Northern Light**

Provider   Northern Light Technology LLC

Description Gives access to a searchable database of over 150 million web pages, and provides searchable access to its Special Collection of more than 5400 full-text sources (abstracts for special collection documents are freely available with a chance to purchase the full text online).

Access   URL   **http://www.northernlight.com/**

Name   **Open Directory Project**

Provider   Netscape

Description Commendable attempt to provide a comprehensive directory of the web, using 15,000 volunteers. Contains nearly a million sites.

Access   URL   **http://dmoz.org/**

Name   **PhoneNet UK Online Phone Directory**

Provider   British Telecommunications plc

Description   Searchable database of UK phone numbers and addresses.

Access   URL   **http://www.bt.co.uk/phonenetuk/**

Name   **PICK**

Provider   Thomas Parry Library, University of Wales Aberystwyth

Description   Quality Internet resources in library and information science, selected by Thomas Parry Library. Contains selected resources organized in a subject directory structure. Keyword searching is available, as is a browsable listing in DDC 21 order.

Access   URL   **http://www.aber.ac.uk/~tplwww/e/pick.html**

Name   **PINAKES**

Provider   Heriot-Watt University

Description   A launchpad for subject information gateways, provides access to major subject gateways worldwide.

Access   URL   **http://www.hw.ac.uk/libWWW/irn/pinakes/pinakes. html**

Name   **Resource Discovery Network**

Provider   Resource Discovery Network Centre (UK)

Description   Co-operative network of information gateways funded by the JISC. Includes access to BIOME (health and medicine and related topics), EMC (engineering, maths and computing) and SOSIG (social sciences, business and law).

Access   URL   **http://www.rdn.ac.uk/**

Name   **Search Tools: a Guide**

Provider   Richard Eskins, Manchester Metropolitan University

Description   Comprehensive guide to search tools: includes links and information. Also includes links to guides to searching the Internet.

Access   URL   **http://www.mmu.ac.uk/h-ss/dic/main/search.htm**

Name   **Search.com**

Provider   CNET, Inc

Description   Enormous list of links to other search services, directories, etc, many of which are searchable from this site.

Access   URL   **http://www.search.com/**

Name   **UK Index**
Provider   UK Index Limited
Description Probably the best option for searching for UK-based sites.
Access   URL   **http://www.ukindex.co.uk/**

Name   **Whoopie!**
Provider   Jason Kim
Description Searchable and browsable index of over one million video and audio files.
Access   URL   **http://www.whoopie.com/**

Name   **WhoWhere?**
Provider   WhoWhere? Inc
Description Searchable database of e-mail, phone and postal addresses.
Access   URL   **http://www.whowhere.lycos.com/**

Name   **World Wide Web Virtual Library**
Provider   WWW Virtual Library
Description A hierarchical subject index of Internet resources worldwide
Comments   The top menu contains an extensive listing of fairly specific subjects with an emphasis on the academic, though commercial, governmental, professional and recreational resources are also referenced. Most main subject-headings link directly to other specialist sites maintained by volunteers. Some are disappointing; others are very rich indeed.
Access   URL   **http://vlib.org/Overview.html**

Name　　**WWLIB: Classified Listing of WWW Pages**

Provider　　Peter Burden

Description　Provides a classified listing of UK web pages.

Comments　The classification (currently experimental) is broadly based on the 20th edition of Dewey, beginning at the single digit level on the home page. Section 0 (generalities, catalogues, newspapers, computing) and Section 3 (social sciences, law, government, society, commerce, education) are particularly rich in UK websites that go well beyond the academic sector. Check Section 0 for servers provided by UK-based hardware and software companies, publishers and the media. Individual pages on the UK Government and HM Treasury servers are incorporated in Section 3, providing a useful resumé of what these cover. Also in Section 3, an extensive list of UK Internet service providers, and in Section 6 (applied science) a good collection of UK industrial companies with websites. This is a good resource to use for an overview of UK initiatives on the web, a sort of Yahoo! equivalent for UK sites.

Access　　URL　　**http://www.scit.wlv.ac.uk/wwlib/**

Name　　**YELL: Yellow Pages UK Home Page**

Provider　　Yellow Pages Division of British Telecommunications plc

Description　Mixture of directory and search service for UK resources. As well as web pages, also includes a searchable electronic yellow pages, a UK film finder, a UK company directory and more.

Access　　URL　　**http://www.yell.co.uk/**

Portals and e-business

Name   Amazon.co.uk
Provider   Amazon.com, Inc

Description   The company blazing a trail that the others are following. It started out with books but has rapidly branched out to a range of other product and service areas.

Access   URLs   **http://www.amazon.co.uk/**
                 http://www.amazon.com/

Name   AOL
Provider   America Online, Inc

Description   By far the largest commercial provider of home Internet access in the world. Started out as a provider of proprietary content only, but soon got swept up in the rush to join in the web.

Access   URLs   **http://www.aol.co.uk/**
                 http://www.aol.com/

Name   Auctionwatch
Provider   AuctionWatch.com

Description   Useful utility which allows the easy tracking of auctions of similar categories or items on different auction sites. At the time of writing being blocked by Ebay.

Access   URL   **http://www.auctionwatch.com/**

Name   Buy.com
Provider   Buy.com (US)

Description   Emphasizes a commitment to the lowest prices anywhere, though it is US-based.

Access   URL   **http://www.buy.com/**

Name   eBay
Provider   eBay Inc

Description   The oldest and best known auction site.

Access   URLs   **http://www.ebay.co.uk/**
                 http://www.ebay.com/

Name	**eToys**
Provider	eToys Inc
Description	Best place for toys. At the time of writing the **co.uk** site was 'coming soon'.
Access	URLs **http://www.etoys.co.uk/** **http://www.etoys.com/**

Name	**Expedia UK**
Provider	Microsoft Corporation
Description	Microsoft's site for booking flight tickets, accommodation and holidays.
Access	URLs **http://www.expedia.co.uk/** **http://www.expedia.com/**

Name	**Itrack**
Provider	Intuitive Systems
Description	E-mail utility which allows the easy tracking of auctions of similar items on different auction sites.
Access	URL **http://www.itrack.com**

Name	**Lastminute.com**
Provider	Lastminute.com
Description	A British e-business which specializes in last-minute deals for holidays, hotels etc.
Access	URL **http://www.lastminute.com/**

Name	**MSN**
Provider	Microsoft Corporation
Description	Microsoft's attempt at a portal. Not yet a major player but slowly gaining on Yahoo! and AOL.
Access	URLs **http://www.msn.co.uk/** **http://www.msn.com/**

Name	**Priceline**
Provider	Priceline.com Inc
Description	Buyers must offer a price for the product/service they want. This site then attempts to find a seller at that price.
Access	URL **http://www.priceline.com/**

Name   **QXL**

Provider   QXL.com

Description   British/European based auction site.

Access   URLs   **http://www.qxl.co.uk/**
                         http://www.qxl.com/

Name   **Travelocity**

Provider   Sabre Inc

Description   Leading site for booking flight tickets, accommodation and holidays.

Access   URLs   **http://www.travelocity.co.uk/**
                         http://www.travelocity.com/

Name   **Yahoo!**

Provider   Yahoo!, Inc

Description   The original portal. Still by far the leader in terms of usage.

Access   URLs   **http://www.yahoo.co.uk/**
                         http://www.yahoo.com/

Information servers and gateways

Name AHDS
Provider Arts and Humanities Data Service (UK)
Description UK nationally funded service to 'collect, preserve and promote re-use of the electronic resources which result from research in the arts and humanities'.
Access URL **http://ahds.ac.uk/**

Name Arts & Letters Daily
Provider Arts & Letters Daily
Description This is the site to refute anyone who complains that the Internet is full of illiterate rubbish. It is a superb compilation of the very latest and best articles from an enormous range of scholarly and erudite publications.
Access URL **http://www.cybereditions.com/aldaily/**

Name The BBS Corner: Introduction to Bulletin Board Systems
Provider Diamond Mine Online Systems, Inc (USA)
Description Overview and typology of bulletin board systems, including extensive listings.
Access URL **http://www.thedirectory.org/diamond/about.htm**

Name BUBL Information Service
Provider BUBL (UK)
Description BUBL acts as both an information service for the library and information professions, and as gateway to Internet resources for the wider academic and research community. As an information service for LIS it includes abstracts and contents pages of a wide selection of LIS and IT journals, news of library research and education, meetings, jobs, new books etc – with a predominantly UK focus. As a gateway, it provides links to an overwhelming number of Internet resources in the UK and worldwide, including electronic journals and texts, worldwide OPACs (via Hytelnet), major networking tools, software and training materials.
Access URL **http://bubl.ac.uk/**

Name   **Free-Nets and Community Networks**
Provider   Peter Scott of Northern Lights Internet Solutions
Description   FreeNet web and telnet sites by country, plus related discussion lists and newsgroups.
Access   URL   **http://www.lights.com/freenet/**

Name   **NISS Information Gateway**
Provider   NISS: National Information Services and Systems (UK)
Description   Aimed at the UK higher education community, and with a wealth of information from and about it, NISS is also a major national gateway to key selected network services of all types, including OPACs, Campus-Wide Information Systems, subject resources, news sources, information technology guides and more. NISS aims to include resources and information which are reliable and of real value to the academic community
Access   URL   **http://www.niss.ac.uk/**

Name   **SciTech Daily Review**
Provider   SciTech Daily Review
Description   A companion site to Arts & Letters Daily. Required daily reading for anyone interested in science and technology.
Access   URL   **http://www.scitechdaily.com/**

Name   **Sensitive Maps**
Provider   School of Computing and Information Technology, University of Wolverhampton
Description   Interactive maps and guides to a wealth of UK sites, including all UK universities, colleges with websites, research-council-funded sites and other sites of general academic and cultural interest that are not directly associated with universities and colleges
Access   URL   **http://scitsc.wlv.ac.uk/ukinfo/uk.map.html**

OPACs and library-based information servers

Name   **CARL Corporation**

Provider   The CARL Corporation

Description Access to over 450 public, academic and school libraries in the USA, plus links to a number of commercial databases (subscribers only), including the massive UnCover (journal contents) database.

Access   URLs   **http://www.carl.org/**
            Telnet **database.carl.org**
            Logout **//EXIT**

Name   **Conservation OnLine**

Provider   Stanford University Libraries, Preservation Department (USA)

Description Documents, mailing list archives and resources of relevance to the conservation of library, archive and museum materials.

Access   URL   **http://palimpsest.stanford.edu/**

Name   **COPAC**

Provider   COPAC Project, Manchester Computing, University of Manchester

Description At the time of writing, the COPAC database contains around 3.5 million records from Cambridge, Oxford, Edinburgh, Glasgow and Leeds university libraries. More university collections will be added.

Access   URL   **http://copac.ac.uk/copac/**

Name   **Digital Libraries: Cataloguing and Indexing of Electronic Resources**

Provider   International Federation of Library Associations (Canada)

Description Provides links to relevant documents and other resources that deal with the cataloguing and indexing of electronic media.

Access   URLs   **http://ifla.inist.fr/II/catalog.htm**
                     http://www.ifla.org/II/catalog.htm

Name   **EARL**

Provider   EARL

Description EARL is a consortium of UK public library authorities and other organizations which aim to make available the Internet to all library users. Offers the excellent 'Ask a librarian' service which provides answers to reference questions by e-mail.

Access   URL   **http://www.earl.org.uk/**

Name   **Hytelnet on the World Wide Web**
Provider   Peter Scott
Comments Reported as closing in 1997 but still not replaced.
Access   URL   **http://www.lights.com/hytelnet**

Name   **Innovative Internet Applications in Libraries**
Provider   Janet Foster
Description Provides links to well-chosen examples of library use of the Internet for a wealth of activities, including bibliographic instruction, cataloguing, collection management, library tours, digital library and electronic publishing projects, public relations and more. Includes some references to relevant publications and examples of Web forms for book requests, interlibrary loans and OPAC searches.
Comments A source of inspiration for libraries who are planning Internet services.
Access   URL   **http://pages.cthome.net/library/innovate.html**

Name   **The Internet Public Library**
Provider   School of Information and Library Studies, University of Michigan (USA)
Description Provides services for children and young people plus links to Internet resources (mostly US) chosen for their interest to public librarians and users. Incorporates an experimental 'ask a question' service for reference questions submitted via e-mail and 'rooms' that can be visited.
Comments Available in graphical and text-only versions. An imaginative experimental concept.
Access   URL   **http://www.ipl.org/**

Name   **LASER**
Provider   LASER: London and South Eastern Library Region
Description Brief information about this library co-operative and associated services and projects, for example VISCOUNT (interlending and bibliographic records), CILLA (acquisition and cataloguing of ethnic language materials), etc.
Access   URL   **http://lirn.viscount.org.uk/laser/**

Name **Library of Congress Home Page**
Provider   Library of Congress (USA)
Description Information at and about the Library of Congress, including a link to their online catalogue and details of how to search it. Also US government, legislative and congressional information and resources for librarians, information professionals and researchers.
Access   URL   **http://lcweb.loc.gov/homepage/**

Name **Libweb**
Provider   Thomas Dowling, University of Washington (USA)
Description A well-organized list of over 3000 library-based web servers from around the world. Also includes a few library-related companies (online service, database and bibliographic software providers).
Comments   Includes useful library web servers from the UK, and a good selection from northern Europe. These give links to OPACs and a wealth of other resources.
Access   URL   **http://sunsite.berkeley.edu/Libweb/**

Name **Portico**
Provider   The British Library
Description Online information about the British Library, principally details of BL structure, functions, events, services and collections and (additionally) information about digitization and networking projects, forthcoming exhibitions, etc. Includes a link to GABRIEL, the web server for Europe's national libraries.
Access   URLs   **http://www.bl.uk/**
                     http://portico.bl.uk/

Name **RLG Home Page**
Provider   Research Libraries Group, Inc (USA)
Description Information from the RLG and links to web servers at member institutions.
Access   URL   **http://www.rlg.org/**

Name   **SALSER: Scottish Academic Library Serials**

Provider   SCURL: Scottish Confederation of University and Research Libraries

Description   A catalogue of journals and other serials held in Scotland's university libraries, the city libraries of Edinburgh and Glasgow, and the National Library of Scotland. Telnet links are also provided to Scottish university OPACs.

Comments   Useful for locating which libraries in a specified region hold a particular journal. Users first select sites before searching by exact journal title, keyword (Boolean) or ISSN. Searches return holdings information.

Access   URL   **http://edina.ed.ac.uk/salser/**

Name   **Technical Processing Tools Online (TPOT)**

Provider   George J. Janczym, UCSD Libraries (USA)

Description   An impressive guide to web resources for acquisitions, cataloguing and serials processing.

Access   URL   **http://tpot.ucsd.edu/**

Name   **UK Higher Education Library Catalogues**

Provider   NISS (UK)

Description   Lists OPACs of higher education and research institutions in the UK. Gives contact, login and basic search instructions for each OPAC and also provides links through to the majority.

Access   URL   **http://www.niss.ac.uk/lis/opacs.html**

Electronic journals, newsletters and alerting services

Name	**Ariadne**
Provider	UKOLN (UK)
Description	Web-based newsletter published every three months, aiming to cover sources and services on the Internet of relevance to librarians, especially the Electronic Libraries Programme (eLib).
Access	URL **http://www.ariadne.ac.uk/**

Name	**BUBL Journals**
Provider	BUBL Information Service (UK)
Description	BUBL itself holds a collection of electronic journals and provides links to major repositories elsewhere. There are also links to directories of e-journals.
Access	URL **http://bubl.ac.uk/journals/**

Name	**CAUSE/EFFECT**
Provider	EDUCAUSE (UK)
Description	Quarterly newsletter for managers and users of information resources in higher education. Also available in printed form
Access	URL **http://cause-www.niss.ac.uk/pub/ce/cause-effect.html**

Name	**Current Cites**
ISSN	1060-2356
Provider	University of California, Berkeley Library (USA)
Description	Provides citations and brief annotations to selected articles from over 30 library and information technology journals (hard copy and electronic), covering optical disc technologies, networks, electronic publishing, hypermedia and multimedia.
Access	URL **http://www.lib.ncsu.edu/stacks/currentc/**
Subscription details	
	E-mail **listserv@library.berkeley.edu**
	Message **sub cites** *your-firstname your-lastname*
	Note Sent automatically to PACS-L and PACS-P subscribers

Name	**DeLiberations**
ISSN	1363-6715
Provider	Educational and Staff Development Unit, London Guildhall University
Description	For educational developers, librarians and academic staff involved in teaching and learning in higher education. Does not have regular issues but is continually updated.
Access	URL **http://www.lgu.ac.uk/deliberations/**

Name	**Directory of Electronic Journals, Newsletters and Academic Discussion Lists**
Provider	Association of Research Libraries (USA)
Description	One of the most extensive, multidisciplinary listings of electronic journals etc on the Internet. Also available for sale in printed format (from the contact given below).
Comments	Electronic journals and newsletters are listed alphabetically by title in two separate sections on the information server (text file). The sections can be searched collectively by keyword. The e-journal section has evolved from the well-known directory first produced by Michael Strangelove at the University of Ottawa. The server also links to the Directory of Scholarly and Professional E-Conferences, compiled by Diane Kovacs and team at Kent State University.
Access	URL **http://arl.cni.org/scomm/edir/**

Name	**D-Lib**
Provider	Defence Advanced Research Projects Agency (DARPA) (USA)
Description	Monthly newsletter reporting on digital library research, especially that from the NSF/DARPA/NASA Digital Library Initiative in the USA
Comments	A UK mirror version of the publication is available from UKOLN.
Access	URLs **http://ukoln.bath.ac.uk/dlib/magazine.html** **http://www.dlib.org/**

Name	**FreePint**
ISSN	1460-7239
Provider	Willco Ltd
Description	Free bi-monthly newsletter distributed via e-mail. Contains information, tips and tricks about using the Internet. Back issues are also available through the website.
Access	URL **http://www.freepint.co.uk/**
Subscription details	
	E-mail **subs@freepint.co.uk**

Name   **Internet Resources Newsletter**

ISSN   1361-9381

Provider   Heriot-Watt University, Internet Resource Centre

Description   Monthly newsletter aiming to raise awareness of selected new resources and services on the Internet.

Access   URL   **http://www.hw.ac.uk/libWWW/irn/irn.html**

Name   **The Katherine Sharp Review**

ISSN   1083-5261

Provider   Graduate School of Library and Information Science, University of Illinois (USA)

Description   Publishes articles within the field of library and information science from student authors.

Access   URL   **http://edfu.lis.uiuc.edu/review/**

Name   **Managing Information**

ISSN   1352-0229

Provider   ASLIB (UK)

Description   Unrestricted online access to the current print issue of Managing Information, an archive of back issues is also available.

Access   URL   **http://www.aslib.co.uk/man-inf/current/**

Name   **NewJour**

Provider   Ann Shumelda Okerson (Yale University) and James J. O'Donnell (University of Pennsylvania) (USA)

Description   List for receiving announcements of electronic journals as they become available. The archive of past announcements is searchable.

Access   URL   **http://gort.ucsd.edu/newjour/**

Subscription details

    E-mail   **listserv@ccat.sas.upenn.edu**

    Message   **subscribe NewJour**

Name   PACS News: Public Access Computer Systems News

ISSN   1050-6004

Provider   University of Houston Libraries (USA)

Description Established in 1990, PACS News is published irregularly with news items related to end-user computer systems in libraries.

Comments   Although many news items originate in the USA, this is a useful newsletter for library software products and system updates. Back issues are available, but only listed by volume and issue.

Access   URL   **http://info.lib.uh.edu/pacsnews.html**

Subscription details

           Note   Sent automatically to PACS-L and PACS-P subscribers

Name   PACS-P: Public Access Computer Systems Publications

Provider   University of Houston Libraries (USA)

Description Subscribers receive all four PACS-L publications (Current Cites, PACS-News, PACS-Review, LITA Newsletter), but not the PACS-L discussions.

Access   URL   **http://info.lib.uh.edu/pacsp.html**

Subscription details

           E-mail **listserv@listserv.uh.edu**

           Message **subscribe pacs-p** *your-firstname your-lastname*

Name   The Public Access Computer Systems Review

ISSN   1048-6542

Provider   Charles W. Bailey, Jr (Editor-in-Chief), University of Houston Libraries (USA)

Description Established in 1989. Publishes articles concerning all aspects of end-user computer systems in libraries. Distributed free of charge via the Internet, with its first five volumes now available in hard copy from American Library Association Library and Information Technology Services.

Comments   Articles can be received automatically by subscribing to PACS-P, or retrieved selectively via the server. Subject and author indexes and author guidelines are also available on the server.

Access   URL   **http://info.lib.uh.edu/pacsrev.html**

Name   Scholarly Journals Distributed via the Web

Provider   Charles W. Bailey, Jr, University of Houston Libraries (USA)

Description An alphabetic, multidisciplinary listing by title, carrying links to – but no further information about – each one.

Access   URL   **http://info.lib.uh.edu/wj/webjour.html**

Name	**Scout Report Homepage**
Provider	Net Scout Services (USA)
Description	Weekly publication of the InterNIC Net Scout project at the University of Wisconsin – Madison, intended to inform researchers and educators of new valuable resources on the Internet. Also produces subject-specific reports for business and economics, science and engineering and the social sciences.
Access	URL **http://scout.cs.wisc.edu/**
	E-mail **listserv@cs.wisc.edu**
	Message **subscribe scout-report**

General reference works

Name   **Altavista Translations**
Provider   Systrans
Description Machine translation tool for five European languages, allows translation from plain text or a URL.
Access   URL   **http://babelfish.altavista.digital.com/**

Name   **Britannica Online**
Provider   Britannica Advanced Publishing, Inc
Description A trial version of the Encyclopaedia Britannica. The full version is only available by subscription. Also provides free access to Britannica's Internet Guide
Access   URL   **http://www.eb.com/**

Name   **Merriam-Webster Online**
Provider   Merriam-Webster, Inc
Description An online version of the Merriam-Webster dictionary and thesaurus.
Access   URL   **http://www.m-w.com/**

Name   **THOR: The Virtual Reference Desk**
Provider   The Libraries of Purdue University (USA)
Description A good composite collection of reference pages from other US academic library servers, plus dictionaries and other reference works.
Access   URL   **http://thorplus.lib.purdue.edu/reference/**

Name   **The Universal Currency Converter™**
Provider   Xenon Laboratories, Inc
Description Provides online conversion for 180 currencies, rates are updated once a minute.
Access   URL   **http://www.xe.net/ucc/**

Name   **The World Wide Web Acronym and Abbreviation Server**
Provider   University of Cork College (Ireland)
Description A searchable index of acronyms and their expansions across a wide range of subjects
Access   URL   **http://www.ucc.ie/info/net/acronyms/**

Name   **Yahoo! Reference**

Provider   Yahoo Inc

Description   Links to a good selection of general reference sources

Access   URLs   **http://www.yahoo.co.uk/Reference/**
                                 http://www.yahoo.com/Reference/

Software and multimedia

Name   **The Archive: SunSITE Northern Europe FTP archive**
Provider   SunSITE Northern Europe; (Department of Computing, Imperial College, London)
Description   A massive archive of software, USENET newsgroups and FAQs, e-journals, multimedia and more. Lists FTP servers worldwide and provides Archie services. Also provides some links to UK-specific networking information.
Access   URLs   **http://src.doc.ic.ac.uk/**
                     ftp://src.doc.ic.ac.uk/

Name   **BIBSOFT: Bibliographic Software Listserv**
Provider   Ruth Lilly Medical Library (USA)
Description   Contains discussions on bibliographic software, and also personal bibliographic software tools (eg Pro-Cite, End Note, Reference Manager).
Access   E-mail   **listserv@listserv.iupui.edu**
              Message   **subscribe bibsoft**

Name   **Digital Librarian: Audio, Video, Rich Media**
Provider   Margaret Vail Anderson
Description   A massive list of links to multimedia resources.
Access   URL   **http://www.servtech.com/~mvail/audio.html**

Name   **EMWAC: European Microsoft Windows NT Academic Centre**
Provider   Datalink Computers, Digital, Microsoft, Research Machines, Sequent and the University of Edinburgh
Description   Comprehensive information on Microsoft products and services, including a rich archive of software utilities, documentation, book-lists, support service information and details of applications software which runs under Windows. Also an 'Internet toolchest' containing server applications on the Windows NT platform. Acts as a mirror site for other hardware and software houses, eg Digital, Netscape.
Access   URLs   **http://www.emwac.ed.ac.uk/**
                     ftp://emwac.ed.ac.uk/

Name   **IFLA Internet and Library Software Archive**

Provider   International Federation of Library Associations (Canada)

Description Aims to provide a careful selection of the 'best' software resources to assist librarians using the Internet. The emphasis will be on client software for MS-Windows and Macintosh machines, and will include library-specific as well as generic Internet applications and utilities. Provides links to several other software archives.

Access   URLs   **http://ifla.inist.fr/II/software.htm**
                    http://ifla.org/II/software.htm

Name   **Internet Explorer UK Mirror**

Provider   Microsoft

Description Contains the latest version of Microsoft's Internet Explorer for Windows platforms and Macintosh.

Access   URL   **http://www.microsoft.com/windows/ie/default.htm**

Name   **Netscape**

Provider   Netscape

Description Software archive, commercial product details, demo versions, documentation and support from Netscape.

Access   URL   **http://home.netscape.com/download/index.html**

Name   **Opera Software**

Provider   Opera Software A/S

Description Software archive, demo versions, documentation and support from Opera.

Access   URL   **http://www.opera.com/**

Name   **Shareware.com**

Type   Software archive; searchable index

Provider   CNET, Inc

Description A massive composite archive, of over 250,000 files, of freeware, shareware, demos, fixes, patches and upgrades. The service provides a search engine (vsl) to search software descriptions. Searches can be restricted to a particular software platform.

Access   URL   **http://www.shareware.com/**

Name   **TUCOWS**

Provider   Tucows.com

Description Name stands for The Ultimate Collection of Winsock Software, and
            it certainly lives up to this! Great source for any Internet application.

Access   URLs   **http://tucows.mirror.ac.uk/**
                    http://tucows.rmplc.co.uk/
                    http://tucows.cableinet.net/
                    http://tucows.enta.net/
                    http://www.tucows.com/

Name   **UK Mirror Service**

Provider   University of Lancaster and the University of Kent with funding
            from JISC (UK)

Description Provides web and FTP mirrors of overseas sites for the UK acade-
            mic community.

Comments   Software is mostly public domain and shareware covering a wide
            range of applications but especially networking. Replaces HENSA as
            the primary mirror service for UK HE.

Access   URL   **http://www.mirror.ac.uk/**

Name   **Updates.com**

Provider   Zdnet

Description Collection of all the latest updates for a wide range of software appli-
            cations. Includes an e-mail notification service for new updates.

Access   URLs   **http://updates.zdnet.co.uk/**
                    http://updates.zdnet.com/

Networking guides and training materials

Name   **Bibliographic Formats for Citing Electronic Information**

Provider   Nancy Crane

Description   Gives advice on how to cite resources on the Internet.

Access   URL   **http://www.uvm.edu/~ncrane/estyles/**

Name   **CNIDR Home Page**

Provider   The Centre for Networked Information Discovery and Retrieval (USA)

Description   CNIDR provides support for information discovery and retrieval applications in particular Z39.50 and Whois++. The server provides software and documentation on the Isite information system.

Access   URL   **http://cnidr.org/**

Name   **The Guide to Network Resource Tools**

Provider   TERENA: Trans European Research and Academic Network Association (Netherlands and Europe)

Description   Clearly written guides to major tools including the web, web search facilities, web conferencing, web authoring, Listserv, Mailbase and USENET. As well as giving an overview of each tool, the guide incorporates details of availability (local and remote clients), intended audience, basic usage and examples.

Comments   Second edition – revised and updated.

Access   URL   **http://www.terena.nl/libr/gnrt/**

Name   **Internet Detective**

Provider   Institute for Learning and Research Technology through the DESIRE Project

Description   An interactive online tutorial for evaluating the quality of information found on the Internet.

Access   URL   **http://www.sosig.ac.uk/desire/internet-detective.html**

Name   **Internet Tourbus**

Provider   Patrick Douglas Crispen and Bob Rankin

Description   Twice weekly virtual tour of the Internet with reviews of sites and tools.

Access   URL   **http://www.tourbus.com/**

Name   **NetLearn: Resources for Learning the Internet**
Provider   Robert Gordon University, Aberdeen
Description   Directory of teaching and learning materials about the Internet.
Access   URL   **http://www.rgu.ac.uk/~sim/research/netlearn/
                       callist.htm**

Name   **Netskills**
Provider   University Computing Service, University of Newcastle
Description   Netskills aims to help the UK higher education community make
              effective use of the Internet for teaching, research and administra-
              tion. A great collection of training packages, notably TONIC (The
              Online Netskills Interactive Tutorial), courses, etc.
Access   URL   **http://www.netskills.ac.uk/**

RESOURCES FROM OTHER ORGANIZATIONS

Government, government-related and international organizations

Name	**BOPCAS: British official publications current awareness service**
Provider	BOPCAS, Ford Collection of British Official Publications, Hartley Library, University of Southampton
Description	BOPCAS provides access to a database of Acts of Parliament, Bills, Green Papers, etc. A subscription option is available.
Comments	Departments and organizations are listed by name and by function (eg Agriculture, Careers). There is also a keyword search facility.
Access	URL **http://www.bopcas.com/**

Name	**CORDIS Homepage**
Provider	European Union
Description	Information on all EU-supported research and development activities, including programmes, publications and research partnerships.
Access	URL **http://www.cordis.lu/**

Name	**EUROPA**
Provider	European Commission
Description	Information on the European Union's goals, institutions and policies.
Access	URL **http://europa.eu.int/**

Name	**FedWorld Information Network**
Provider	NTIS: National Technical Information Service (USA)
Description	US Government information servers, FTP and telnet sites organized by subject. Also reports, databases and software from NTIS.
Access	URLs **http://www.fedworld.gov/** **ftp://ftp.fedworld.gov/**

Name   **I*M Europe Home Page**
Provider   DG XIII (EU)
Description   Information about the EU and European Parliament, notably EU
              programmes and calls for proposals related to the European infor-
              mation market and the INFO 2000 programme.
Access   URL   **http://www.echo.lu/**

Name   **Open.gov.uk**
Provider   CCTA: Central Computer and Telecommunications Authority
              (UK)
Description   Acts as a repository for information supplied by a large number of
              UK government departments and agencies, with links to those who
              have their own information servers (mostly websites). These range
              from the Central Office of Information to the Charity Commission,
              the British Council to the Building Research Establishment. The
              full texts of citizen's charters are rapidly being added as is informa-
              tion from local government as it becomes available.
Comments   Departments and organizations are listed by name and by function
              (eg Agriculture, Careers). There is also a keyword search facility.
Access   URL   **http://www.open.gov.uk/**

Name   **UNDP: United Nations Development Programme**
Provider   United Nations System
Description   UN documents, conferences, directories etc.
Access   URL   **http://www.undp.org/**

Booksellers, publishers and the media

Name   **The BBC Home Page**

Provider   BBC: British Broadcasting Corporation

Description   TV and radio programme schedules; programme information, fact-sheets and some transcripts; current affairs; news reviews and analysis; BBC Education resources; and much more from and about the BBC.

Access   URL   **http://www.bbc.co.uk/**

Name   **Book Industry Communication's Bookish Home Page**

Provider   Book Industry Communication (UK)

Description   A central access point for information from the UK book industry, plus links to relevant international sites. Includes UK and Irish booksellers, library suppliers, subscription agents, library systems suppliers, UK and European English-language publishers who are providing information via the network.

Access   URL   **http://www.bic.org.uk/**

Name   **Book Web Home Page**

Provider   American Booksellers Association

Description   News, discussion and information about books, authors and the US book industry.

Access   URL   **http://www.ambook.org/**

Name   **BUBL LINK: 070.5 Publishing**

Provider   BUBL Information Service (UK)

Description   A collection of links to booksellers and publishers (conventional and electronic), both US and UK.

Access   URL   **http://link.bubl.ac.uk/publishing/**

Name   **Internetbookinfo.com**

Provider   Internet Book Information Center, Inc

Description   Provides good links to a wealth of (mostly US) publishing and bookselling resources on the Internet, including awards and bestsellers, author information, book reviews, poetry archives, USENET newsgroups as well as directories of publishers and booksellers themselves.

Access   URL   **http://www.internetbookinfo.com/**

Name   **Internet Bookshop Homepage**
Provider   W H Smith
Description   A local competitor for *Amazon*.
Access   URL   **http://www.bookshop.co.uk/**

Name   **Media UK Internet Directory**
Provider   Media UK
Description   E-mail contact addresses and links to UK media-related sites, including TV, radio, newspapers (local and national) and magazines.
Access   URL   **http://www.mediauk.com/directory/**

Name   **Publishers' Catalogues Home Page**
Provider   Peter Scott, Northern Lights Internet Solutions Ltd
Description   Publishers' information servers and catalogues from around the world, listed by country.
Access   URL   **http://www.lights.com/publisher/**

Name   **The World Wide Web Virtual Library: Publishers**
Provider   Jonathan Bowen, Oxford University Computing Laboratory
Description   An extensive alphabetical list of Internet-accessible publishers from around the world. Also provides links to selected online bookstores and to broadcasters (listed by country).
Access   URL   **http://www.comlab.ox.ac.uk/archive/publishers. html**

Commercial online information retrieval services

Name **Bell & Howell: Information and Learning**

Provider   Bell & Howell

Description Bell & Howell (formerly UMI) provides bibliographic, microfilming and distribution services for doctoral and master's theses and dissertations produced worldwide. There is a wealth of information and guidelines about the dissertations services. Additionally the web server contains information about additional products, services and events, including document delivery, electronic products and serials on microform.

Access   URL   **http://www.umi.com/**

Name **BIDS**

Provider   BIDS: Bath Information and Data Services (UK)

Description BIDS supports end-user access to a number of commercial online bibliographic databases, including ERIC (Educational Resources Information Centre), British Education Index, Inspec (physics, chemistry and computing) and Compendex (engineering).

Comments   Information about the service and databases is available on the web server. Although established for UK academic institutions, subscriptions to some of the databases are available more widely. There is a Mailbase discussion list for BIDS users (lis-bids-users).

Access   URL   **http://www.bids.ac.uk/**

            Telnet **bids.ac.uk** (subscribers only)

Name **Blaise Web**

Provider   The British Library

Description Hosts the major British Library catalogues and MARC files as well as related databases from other suppliers.

Comments   Users are required to register to use the service, general information is posted to the lis-bl-blaiseline list on Mailbase.

Access   URL   **http://blaiseweb.bl.uk/**

            Telnet **blaise.bl.uk** (subscribers only)

Name   **DataStar Web**

Provider   Knight-Ridder Information

Description A multidisciplinary online host, with an emphasis on healthcare, biomedical, biotechnology and business information. The server provides brief, keyword-searchable descriptions of all Data-Star databases, listed by their codes.

Access   URL   **http://ds.datastarweb.com/ds/products/datastar/ds. htm**

Name   **Dialog Corporation**

Provider   Dialog Corporation plc

Description There are hundreds of databases on DIALOG, covering all disciplines. Information about both online and ondisc (CD-ROM) information products and services, including associated publications, such as the Dialog Database Catalog and Price List, are available on the server. Database descriptions can be browsed by subject or searched by keyword.

Comments DIALOG news and updates are also distributed to subscribers of the majordomo@www.dialog.com mailing list.

Access   URL   **http://www.dialog.com/**

             Telnet   **dialog.com** (subscribers only)

Name   **EINS Databases**

Provider   European Information Network Services

Description A consortium of predominantly scientific and technical databases.

Access   URL   **http://www.eins.org/**

Name   **European Patent Office**

Provider   European Patent Office (Austria)

Description Information from and about the EPO (eg patent granting procedures), links to servers from other patent offices around the world, plus details of commercial databases containing patent information.

Access   URL   **http://www.european-patent-office.org/**

Name   **ISO Online**

Provider   ISO: International Standards Organization (Switzerland)

Description   Includes information about ISO, its structure, membership and activities. Makes freely available a catalogue of all ISO standards (including drafts), handbooks and other publications.

Comments   Standards are listed by subject according to the International Classification for Standards. The catalogue can also be searched by text keyword and standard number. Pricing and ordering information is available, although online ordering is not supported.

Access   URL   **http://www.iso.ch/**

Name   **LEXIS-NEXIS Communication Center**

Provider   LEXIS-NEXIS

Description   News and legal information from the USA and around the world. The server includes (amongst others) a guide to system commands, and an alphabetical list of Lexis/Nexis files.

Access   URL   **http://www.lexis-nexis.com/**

            Telnet   **nex.lexis-nexis.com** (subscribers only)

Name   **OCLC: Online Computer Library Centre**

Provider   OCLC: Online Computer Library Centre, Inc (USA)

Description   *OCLC First Search* provides access to OCLC's online union catalogue of member libraries (World Cat), other OCLC databases and some well-known databases from other suppliers. Information and limited OCLC documentation are available on the server.

Access   URL   **http://www.oclc.org/**

            Telnet   **fscat.oclc.org** (subscribers only)

Name   **SilverPlatter Worldwide Library**

Provider   SilverPlatter Information, Inc

Description   Details of SilverPlatter's CD-ROM and related information products, training and support services, software and Internet-related activities.

Access   URLs   **http://www.silverplatter.com/**

                     ftp://ftp.silverplatter.com/

Name   **STN International**

Provider   STN: Scientific and Technical Information Network (Germany)

Description   Over 100 scientific and technical databases, with a strong emphasis on chemical information.

Access   URL   **http://www.fiz-karlsruhe.de/stn.html**

        Telnet   **stn.fiz-karlsruhe.de** (subscribers only)

Name   **UnCover Web 2.0**

Provider   CARL Corporation (USA); BH Blackwell Group (UK)

Description   Offers tables of contents and a document delivery service for approximately 18,000 journals. Providing multidisciplinary and international journal coverage, this is one of the largest and most up-to-date databases of its kind.

Comments   Documents can be ordered online and delivered by fax. Contents pages of selected journals can be delivered to individuals' electronic mailboxes. There is a fee for this and for every document ordered, but no charge for searching the database (by author, keyword or journal title). Further information about UnCover and other CARL services is available on the web server. Use telnet to connect directly to the database. (UK academic libraries normally access via the BIDS subscription service).

Access   URL   **http://uncweb.carl.org/**

        Telnet   **database.carl.org**

        Path   **1: Uncover**

        Logout   **//EXIT**

Name   **Winstar Telebase**

Provider   Winstar Telebase, Inc

Description   Offers access to more than 500 online databases, including many well known business sources. Subscription details are available on the server, as well as brief database descriptions.

Access   URL   **http://www.telebase.com/**

        Telnet   **easynet.telebase.com** (subscribers only)

Library and information education

Name   **BAILER WWW Server**

Provider   British Association for Information and Library Education and Research

Description Includes information from and about BAILER and its committees, and a directory of UK departments of library and information studies. Also contains links to directories of LIS departments in other parts of the world.

Access   URL   **http://www.staff.livjm.ac.uk/busjofar/bailer/**

Name   **BECTa**

Provider   British Educational Communications and Technology Agency (UK)

Description Formerly known as the National Council for Educational Technology (NCET). It contains a wealth of information on educational technology, including BECTa publications and project details. Also provides links to other education-specific information servers (mostly UK).

Comments   A highly functional menu structure allows access to information by user orientation/needs. This includes access by user's role (eg parent/librarian); educational level (eg primary/secondary); specific subject (eg GNVQs); Type of technology (eg computer software) etc.

Access   URL   **http://www.becta.org.uk/**

Name   **CERLIM**

Provider   Centre for Research in Library and Information Management (UK)

Description Undertakes research into library and information services' operational work.

Access   URL   **http://www.mmu.ac.uk/h-ss/cerlim/**

Name   **CRISTAL-ED**

Provider   School of Information and Library Studies, University of Michigan with the support of the Kellogg Foundation (USA)

Description Information from a five-year project (commencing 1995) which aims to 'reinvent' the core curriculum for LIS to meet changing needs and to define new LIS specializations.

Access   URL   **http://www.si.umich.edu/cristaled/**

Subscription details

         E-mail   **majordomo@si.umich.edu**

         Message **subscribe cristal-ed**

Name **CTI Home Page**
Provider CTI: Computers in Teaching Initiative (UK)
Description The CTI is funded by the Higher Education Funding Councils, and
provides information and support on the use of computers for teaching in HE via a number of specialist centres dealing with different
disciplines (of which library and information studies is one). The
server provides general information from CTI headquarters, including events and publications, and links to all the various subject centres.
Comments The CTI programme was expected to end in December 1999 and be
replaced by a new Learning Teaching and Support Network.
Access URL **http://www.cti.ac.uk/**

Name **CTILIS Home Page**
Provider Computers in Teaching Initiative, Centre for Library and
Information Studies (UK)
Description The server carries (mostly) back issues of newsletters from CTILIS,
the contents of which include reviews and reports of software pack-
ages used in teaching. Also links to other resources for LIS educators
Comments The CTI programme was expected to end in December 1999 and be
replaced by a new Learning Teaching and Support Network
Access URL **http://info.lboro.ac.uk/departments/ls/cti/**

Name **The Library and Information Commission**
Provider Library and Information Commission (UK)
Description Provides advice and support on library and information issues as well
as funds for LIS research in the UK.
Access URL **http://www.lic.gov.uk/**

Name **The Times Higher Education Supplement**
Provider The Times Higher Education Supplement (UK)
Description Headlines, introductions, digests and summaries of items in the current issue only of the newspaper. Also includes job advertisements
(before the Friday paper), booklists and mailing lists for topical discussions.
Access URL **http://www.thesis.co.uk/**

LIS and related professional associations

Name American Library Association Home Page
Provider American Library Association
Description Information about the membership, constitution, activities, publications, etc of the ALA. Policy and consultative documents available.
Access URL **http://www.ala.org/**

Name Aslib
Provider Aslib, The Association for Information Management (UK)
Description Information about the membership, activities, special interest groups, publications and training courses available.
Access URL **http://www.aslib.co.uk/**

Name Association of Research Libraries
Provider Association of Research Libraries (USA)
Description ARL membership list, reports and publications.
Access URL **http://arl.cni.org/**

Name BCS Net
Provider British Computer Society
Description BCS structure, events, awards, publications, etc.
Access URL **http://www.bcs.org.uk/**

Name IEE Home Page
Provider Institution of Electrical Engineers (UK)
Description Professional, publishing and information services from the IEE.
Access URL **http://www.iee.org.uk/**

Name IFLANET
Provider IFLA: International Federation of Library Associations (Canada)
Description Provides information about IFLA (structure, membership, publications, grants, conferences, etc). Also provides compilations of other documents and resources of generic interest to the library world, including copyright and intellectual property; cataloguing and indexing of electronic resources; interlibrary loan, document delivery and resource sharing information; IT standards and organizations; and library and related information policy statements.
Access URLs **http://ifla.inist.fr/**
http://www.ifla.org/

Name   **Institute of Information Scientists**
Provider   The Institute of Information Scientists (UK)
Description Information about the Institute, its newsletter *Inform*, how to
            become a member, etc.
Access   URL   **http://www.iis.org.uk/**

Name   **The Library Association**
Provider   The Library Association (UK)
Description Information about events, training courses etc, including LA
            branches and special interest groups. Also includes a regularly
            updated web page for Library Association Publishing, including a
            full list of publications, author information and book reviews.
Access   URL   **http://www.la-hq.org.uk/**

Name   **LISU**
Provider   The Library and Information Statistics Unit, Loughborough
            University
Description Statistical information about libraries, provides annual statistics
            tables including expenditure, acquisitions, usage, etc.
Access   URL   **http://www.lboro.ac.uk/departments/dis/lisu/lisuhp.
            html**

Name   **SIGIR Information Server**
Provider   Association for Computing Machinery: Special Interest Group on
            Information Retrieval (USA)
Description Information about ACM SIGIR plus links to a selection of other
            related SIGs, professional societies and resources.
Access   URL   **http://acm.org/sigir/**

Name   **UKOLN Information Service**
Provider   UKOLN: The UK Office for Library and Information Networking
Description Provides information about UKOLN itself (eg research, publica-
            tions, activities etc) and is host to a number of library – and infor-
            mation-related sites and services. Has good links to related research
            activities in networked information retrieval.
Access   URL   **http://www.ukoln.ac.uk/**

RESOURCES LINKED TO PART 3

Utilities

Name   **Accessing the Internet by E-Mail: Guide to Offline Internet Access**

Provider   Gerald E Boyd

Description How to access FTP, Gopher, Archie, Veronica, Finger, USENET, Whois, Netfind, WAIS and the world wide web via e-mail.

Comments   E-mail access is no substitute for the 'real thing', but this gives valuable guidance if e-mail is all you have.

Access   E-mail   **mailbase@mailbase.ac.uk**

            Message   **send lis-iis e-access-inet.txt**

Name   **Alexa**

Provider   Amazon.com

Description Companion browser service which provides related links and statistics about the sites you visit. The program can be downloaded freely from the Alexa site.

Access   URL   **http://www.alexa.com/**

Name   **Anonymous Remailers**

Provider   Andre Bacard

Description FAQ (regularly posted to news.answers) which provides a clear explanation of remailers, and includes a reference to a list of reliable remailers.

Access   URL   **http://www.andrebacard.com/remail.html**

Name   **Anonymous Surfing**

Provider   Community ConneXion, Inc

Description Removes the information that browsers offer about their users (eg name, e-mail address, date and time on user's system, etc). Also contains links to other sites related to security.

Access   URL   **http://www.anonymizer.com/**

Name   **BrowserWatch: Plug-In Plaza**

Provider   internet.com Corp

Description Lists web browser plug-ins, both by type and computer platform.

Access   URL   **http://browserwatch.internet.com/plug-in.html**

Name **comp.compression FAQ**

Provider   Jean-loup Gailly

Description   Useful guide to file types and file compression/decompression software. Contains links to the actual software required for dealing with different compressed files.

Access: URLs   **http://www.lib.ox.ac.uk/internet/news/faq/comp. compression.html**

http://www.faqs.org/faqs/compression-faq/part1/

Name **Cryptography**

Provider   Francis Litterio

Description   An exhaustive compilation of information relating to the important area of cryptographic applications for networks. Contains details on where to get the PGP (Pretty Good Privacy) package and how to use it. Part of the *WWW Virtual Library* (p93).

Access   URL   **http://world.std.com/~franl/crypto.html**

Name **FaxMe**

Provider   Nildram Ltd

Description   A free fax-to-e-mail service. People can send you faxes, which are re-routed to your e-mail mailbox.

Access   URL   **http://www.faxme.co.uk/**

Name **Freedrive**

Provider   Nextec Communications Corporation

Description   A free service providing up to 20 Mb of personal disk storage, accessible via the Internet.

Access   URL   **http://www.freedrive.com/**

Name **Hotmail**

Provider   Microsoft Corporation

Description   Free web-based e-mail accounts.

Access   URL   **http://www.hotmail.com/**

Name **HyperText Markup Language (HTML): Working and Background Materials**

Provider   W3C

Description   Includes an explanation of HTML markup tags, specifications and user guides plus details of the development of HTML.

Access   URL   **http://www.w3.org/MarkUp/**

Name   Jargon File Resources
Provider   Eric S. Raymond
Description   A well-organized list of jargon used by computer subcultures. Contains links to related documents on hackers and hacking.
Access   URL   http://www.tuxedo.org/~esr/jargon/

Name   LINX Looking Glass
Provider   London Internet Exchange (LINX)
Description   Online tool that will perform traceroute.
Access   URL   http://www.linx.net/cgi-bin/lg.pl?LINX-London

Name   McAffee.com Anti Virus Center
Provider   McAffee.com Corp
Description   Information and help on identifying and removing computer viruses.
Access   URL   http://www.mcaffee.com/centers/anti-virus/

Name   Mind-It
Provider   NetMind, Inc
Description   Alerting service that informs you when a web page has changed (you can choose to be notified by e-mail, via the web, pager or personal digital assistant).
Access   URL   http://mindit.netmind.com/

Name   The Net: User Guidelines and Netiquette
Provider   Arlene Rinaldi
Description   The URL gives links to this document in HTML form and to related material on site computer-use policies.
Access   URL   http://www.fau.edu/rinaldi/netiquette.html

Name   NewsNow
Provider   NewsNow Publishing
Description   News aggregation site catering for a UK audience. It keeps users informed of all the latest stories being added to the top news and information sites on the web. Its goal is to take users to the widest range of quality online news sources from a single, convenient location. Updates every five minutes.
Access   URL   http://www.newsnow.co.uk/

Name — Newzbot

Provider — James W. Abendschan

Description — Gives an up-to-date listing of public access news servers. These are unfortunately not very reliable or fast.

Access — URL — **http://jammed.com/~newzbot/**

Name — Onelist

Provider — ONElist, Inc

Description — Allows the setting up of an e-mail list on any topic. It already has a collection of thousands of e-mail lists.

Access — URL — **http://www.onelist.com/home.html**

Name — Oneview

Provider — Oneview

Description — A free service for storing bookmarks/favourites online, where they will be easily accessible.

Access — URL — **http://www.oneview.com/**

Name — Postmaster

Provider — Bibliotech

Description — Free web-based e-mail accounts.

Access — URL — **http://www.postmaster.co.uk/**

Name — SearchEngineWatch

Provider — internet.com Corp

Description — Useful and informative guide to search engines; provides overviews of the major search engines, plus tutorials, reviews and tips.

Access — URL — **http://www.searchenginewatch.com/**

Name — UK Tuner

Provider — Nottingham University

Description — Definitive listing of UK-sourced radio, television and web casts.

Access — URL — **http://urn.nott.ac.uk/tuner/**

Name — The Unofficial Smiley Dictionary

Provider — EFF: Electronic Frontier Foundations (USA)

Description — A long list of smileys (emoticons). Part of the EFF's (Extended) Guide to the Internet.

Access — URLs — **http://www.sbu.ac.uk/guides/eegtti/eeg_286.html**
http://www.eff.org/papers/eegtti/eeg_286.html

Name   **Urban Legends and Folklore**

Provider   About.com

Description   Lots of fascinating stories of the strange side of the Internet, which warn of the many e-mail scams in existence.

Access   URL   **http://urbanlegends.about.com/**

Name   **The Webcam Resource**

Provider   Arizona Internet Services

Description   Well-organized listing covering web cams by type and location, as well as advice on how to set up a web cam.

Access   URL   **http://www.webcamresource.com/**

Name   **Whois**

Provider   Network Solutions, Inc

Description   Provides a search of the main domain name registry.

Access   URL   **http://www.networksolutions.com/cgi-bin/whois/ whois**

INDEX

Index